THE ULTIMATE DIRTY JOKE BOOK

THE ULTIMATE DIRTY JOKE BOOK

Mike Oxbent & Harry P. Ness

Ulysses Press

Published in the U.S. by Ulysses Press
                P.O. Box 3440
                Berkeley, CA 94703
                www.ulyssespress.com

This edition first published as *The Ultimate Book of Filthy Jokes* in Great Britain in 2005 by Robson Books, The Chrysalis Building, Bramley Road, London W10 6SP

ISBN10: 1-56975-581-7
ISBN13: 978-1-56975-581-5
Library of Congress Control Number 2006907935

Printed in Canada by Transcontinental Printing

10 9 8 7 6 5 4 3 2 1

Editorial: Elyce Petker
Production: Matt Orendorff
Cover design: Double R Design

Distributed by Publishers Group West

Contents

Preface

Hello. Welcome to *The Ultimate Dirty Joke Book*—a collection of jokes that have been deemed the dirtiest of the dirty, the most disgustingly rude of the disgustingly rude, *la phlegm de la phlegm*. These are the jokes that would make a sailor wince, the editor of the *National Enquirer* blush and Howard Stern reach for his pen to compose a strongly worded complaint about the language. They have been hand-picked (by particularly grubby hands), edited to remove anything less than utterly obscene and set in print by one of the most foul-mouthed printers in Christendom. Yes, there is very little that isn't smutty and rude about this volume. In fact, you should see what we're doing, wearing, sitting on and smearing each other with as we write this. So if you don't like dirty jokes, this probably isn't the book for you. And if it is the book for you, you should be ashamed of yourself. I'm afraid you have thus revealed yourself to the world to be some kind of dirty joke pervert or, as the medical profession would put it, a humor-sexual.

The History of Dirty Jokes

The Ultimate Dirty Joke Book is the most recent flowering of a proud, age-old tradition of smut-based humor in written form. What is believed to be the first dirty joke collection was written on the walls of an Egyptian tomb in 2345 B.C. Fifteen off-color gags can be found on the east wall, the least revolting of which can be translated as follows:

Why did Nefertiti stick the [frog] [ibis] [wavy line] [wavy line] up Pharaoh's [hippo] [ibis] [basket] [question mark] Because she caught him wiggling his [eye] [stork] [serving maid] [weasel] with his [rice flail] [rice flail] [jackal head] in a crocodile's [baboon] [hand] [eye] [frog] [exclamation mark] [exclamation mark].

In Europe sordid jokes were often written out by monks, who then sent them to other monasteries via pigeon post (a forerunner of the modern e-mail system of dirty humor distribution). It is thought that a collection of these individual jokes was put together by William Caxton in 1475 as an appendix to his first illustrated book *Ye Bigge Book of Twattes*. Unfortunately all copies of this volume were destroyed by the Bishop of Durham following a dispute about royalties (the Bishop claimed he had copyright on at least half the material). The only joke to survive the flames was the following dirty gag, which some believe was written by Chaucer:

And ther also wass a manne who wass an homosexualle, Who wass a-sitting in a tubbe with his beste friendes alle, A-playing with themselves, and merrily stirring up a lather, Whan suddenly tha came a white blobbe a-floating in the watter. Than up-spoke the first homosexualle to the assembled companye, "Which manne in this tubbe just farted? It certainly wass not me!"

The following centuries saw an increasing number of tawdry humor titles being printed in the U.K. The most famous collection of Elizabethan jokes was *Master Puck's Smutty Jests and Japes* by William Shakespeare (not *the* William Shakespeare obviously, another one), who was also responsible for the best-selling *Another Bigge Book of Twattes*. There was a hiatus in the crude joke book industry during the Commonwealth when Cromwell banned everything except knock-knock jokes, but after the Restoration, London was once again able to chuckle at the dirty stories in books such as *The Lamentable Almanack*, *Dr. Mipsy's Vile and Voluptuous Villainy* and *Yet Another Bigge Book of Twattes*.

Notable titles of the Victorian period include *The Lollard's Lubricious Laughter Library of Libidinous Lewdness*, *Professor McNibblet's Composite of Cheeky Chuckles* and *The Big Book of Ankles*. While in the early twentieth century the great artist Picasso shocked audiences across Europe with the exhibitions of his blue joke period, including such material as: "What do you call a woman with three breasts? Anything you like—her ears are coming out of her ass!" Since then, hundreds if not thousands of dirty joke collections have been printed. There is, however, one thing previous collections of crude jocularity have in common: They are all rubbish. This book (the one you're reading now), however, is really, really good. Yes, this is *the* best crude joke book there is and you're very clever to have bought it. So, please reward yourself in whatever manner you feel is suitable—ideally once you've left the bookstore.

Dirty Joke Book Etiquette

There are situations in which it is very probably—if not almost certainly—unwise to quote from *The Ultimate Dirty Joke Book*:

For example, when being introduced to a new girlfriend's parents for the first time, you might want to think twice about launching into the story of the gentleman of alternative persuasion who hides his life partner's birthday surprise in a particularly unusual place. Similarly, if you happen to be introduced to the President, he's probably not going to want to hear the story of the lady who does the splits in the shower and suctions herself to the tiles—not from you, anyway! Other occasions on which it might be best to avoid quoting directly from the material contained herein include:

- During confession
- On your first day as leader of a Brownie pack
- While canvassing door-to-door for any of the leading political parties
- While performing a baptism
- While in court announcing the verdict of the jury
- While being interviewed on live television
- During a funeral address
- During any religious ceremonies—let's get that straight at least
- While performing an orthopedic massage on an elderly relative
- While carrying the drinks in for your boss during an important business meeting that you are otherwise not party to
- And, if you are a medical professional, during a major surgical operation in which your patient has accidentally remained conscious.

Finally, it should be pointed out that the dirty jokes in this book are not really jokes at all. In actuality they are all genuine real events that have actually occurred in the life of one of the authors. If you rearrange the contents of the book into the correct chronological sequence, you will find they form this said gentleman's complete autobiography to date and his true identity will be revealed unto you [Clue: He is a prominent member of Congress].

Accidents and Disasters

A woman is taking a shower when she slips, does the splits and suctions herself to the floor. She yells out for her husband, who tries to pull her up. After a few minutes of struggling he gives up, "It's no good," he says. "You're stuck tight." "Well, get a hammer and chisel," replies the woman. "Break the floor tiles." "Hang on," says the husband. "I'll tell you what: I'll play with your tits for a few minutes—that might get you wet enough to slide you out into the kitchen." "How's that going to help me?" asks the woman. "It won't," replies her husband. "But the tiles in the kitchen are a hell of a lot cheaper than the ones in here!"

·····

Two male firefighters are having energetic anal sex in a smoke-filled room. Their chief bursts in through the door and shouts, "What the hell are you bastards up to?" One of the firefighters looks up and replies, "Kowalski is suffering from smoke inhalation, sir!" The chief asks, "Well, why aren't you giving him mouth-to-mouth resuscitation?" "I did, sir," replies the firefighter. "How the hell do you think this shit got started?"

·····

A woman is on the balcony of her 17th floor condominium when a gust of wind blows her over the railing. As she passes the 14th floor a man standing on his balcony catches her in his arms. "Do you suck?" he asks. "No," she replies. So the man drops her. As she passes the 12th floor another man catches her. "Do you screw?" he asks. "No," she replies, and the second man also drops her. A man on the 8th floor catches her and the woman shouts, "I'll do anything—I suck, I screw...!" The man replies, "Jesus, what a slut!" and drops her.

• • • • •

Harry takes a phone call from a doctor in the emergency room. The doctor says, "I'm sorry, but your wife has been in a car crash. I have bad news and good news: The bad news is that she's lost the use of her arms and legs. She'll need your help with eating and going to the bathroom for the rest of her life." "Oh, my God!" replies Harry. "So what's the good news?" The doctor says, "I'm kidding—she's dead."

Addiction

A man has a terrible addiction to cigars and goes to his doctor to try and find a cure. The doctor recommends a drastic form of aversion therapy. "When you go to bed tonight, take one of your cigars, unwrap it and stick it completely up your asshole," says the doctor. "Next day remove the cigar, rewrap it and place it back with all the others so you can't tell which one it is. The aversion is obvious: You won't dare smoke any of them, not knowing which is the treated cigar." "Thanks, Doc. I'll give it a go," says the man, and away he goes. Three weeks later the man comes back. "You're *still* an addict?" asks the doctor. "I'm surprised—it's usually a very effective cure." "It *was* effective," replies the man. "I don't smoke cigars anymore, but now I can't go to sleep without a cigar shoved up my ass!"

••••••

Three men meet with their doctor: one is an alcoholic, another a chain-smoker and the third a homosexual. The doctor, addressing all three, says, "If any of you indulge in your vices one more time, you will die." The men leave the doctor's office and walk toward the subway. They pass a bar and the alcoholic, hearing the music and smelling the beer, can't stop himself—he *must* have a drink. All three go into the bar, where the alcoholic has a shot of whisky. He downs his drink in one gulp and falls off his stool, stone dead. His companions realize how seriously they must take the doctor's words. They're about to leave when they spot a lit cigarette, smoldering on the floor. The homosexual looks at the chain-smoker and says, "If you bend over to pick that up, we're both screwed!"

Adultery

A man comes home from work, walks into his bedroom and finds a man having sex his wife. He asks, "What the hell are you doing?" His wife turns to the man and says, "See, I told you he was stupid!"

•••••

A woman discovers her husband is having an affair. She kills him and decides to bury his body in the countryside. She hauls his naked body into the trunk of her car, but when she slams the trunk shut, she accidentally severs his penis. She picks up the dismembered organ and puts in on the dashboard. The woman then drives off, but she's under such tremendous mental strain that her erratic steering soon attracts the attention of a police car. She speeds up to avoid the cops, but realizes they're gaining on her. Suddenly she remembers that her husband's penis is sitting on the dashboard in full view, so she flings it out through the sunroof. The penis flies through the air before hitting the windshield of the police car and bouncing off into the night. "She's driving like a maniac," exclaims one of the policemen. "Never mind her," replies the other cop. "Did you see the size of the cock on that fly?"

•••••

A cop gets off work four hours early and arrives home at one in the morning. Not wanting to wake his wife, he undresses in the dark, creeps into the bedroom and starts to climb into bed. His wife asks, "Darling, would you go down to the all-night drugstore and get me some aspirin? I've got a splitting headache." "Certainly, honey," replies the cop and, feeling his way across the dark room, he gets dressed and walks over to the drugstore. When the cop arrives at the drugstore, the pharmacist looks at him in surprise, "Don't I know you?" he asks. "I thought you were a policeman?" "I am a policeman," replies the cop. "What about it?" "Just curious," replies the pharmacist. "I just wondered what the hell you're doing dressed up like a fire chief!"

•••••

A husband suspects his wife is having an affair. He needs to go on a long business trip, so he sets a trap for her. He puts a bowl of cream under the bed and from the bed-springs he suspends a spoon. He's calculated that his wife's weight on the bed will not drop the spoon into the cream.

But if there's any more weight than that, the spoon will fall into the cream and he'll be able to see it on his return. He comes home several days later and the first thing he does is reach under the bed and retrieve the bowl—which is now full of butter.

•••••

A man comes home and finds his best friend in bed with his wife. "You bastard!" he exclaims. "I've known you since school—you were my best man and my son's godfather, I gave you a job, I lent you money… Stop doing that when I'm talking to you!"

•••••

A man finds a woman crying on a park bench and asks her what's the matter. "My husband's been caught having sex with one of his patients. He's cheated on me and now it looks like he'll be fired." "That's terrible," replies the man. "But look on the bright side, news like that can't get any worse." "Oh, yes it can," sobs the woman. "He's a vet!"

•••••

A man walks into a bar and orders a beer. "Coming right up, sir," replies the bartender. "That'll be one penny." "One penny for a beer?" asks the man. "That's incredible! How much is the food in this place?" "We've got a great steak dinner," says the bartender. "You get a two-pound steak, potatoes, salad and a dessert for three pennies." "That's amazing," says the man. "How do manage to make a profit with such low prices?" "You'd have to ask the owner that," replies the bartender, "but he's not here right now, he's upstairs with my wife." "What's he doing with your wife?"

asks the man. The bartender replies, "The same as I'm doing to his business!"

•••••

A private detective reports back to his female client. "Yesterday I followed your husband to two bars on Elm Street, a singles club on Maple and finally to the Hump-more Motel," he says. "I see," says the woman. "And do you think that's enough grounds for divorce?" "I'm not sure," replies the detective. "After all, he was following you at the time!"

•••••

A studly guy walks into his local bar and orders a drink. He looks worried and the bartender asks him if anything is wrong. "Some pissed-off husband wrote to me and said he'd kill me if I didn't stop screwing his wife." "So why don't you just stop?" asks the bartender. "I can't," replies the stud. "He didn't sign his name!"

•••••

A woman is in bed with her boyfriend when she hears her husband's car pull into the driveway. "Hurry!" she yells to him. "Grab your clothes and jump out the window!" The boyfriend looks out the window and replies, "I can't jump out there—it's raining!" "Jump or he'll kill us both!" shouts the woman. So the boyfriend grabs his clothes and jumps. As he sprints down the street, he discovers he's run right into the middle of a town marathon. He starts running alongside the others and, though naked with his clothes tucked under his arm, tries to blend in as best he can. One of the runners asks him, "Do you always run in the nude?" The boyfriend replies, "Oh, yes, it feels so good with the air blowing over your skin." "And do you always run carrying your clothes with you?" asks the runner. "Yes," answers the boyfriend. "That way I can get dressed at the end of the run and not catch a chill." The runner then asks, "And do you always wear a condom?" The boyfriend replies, "Only if it's raining!"

•••••

George got home and found a man in bed with his wife. Furious, he asks the man, "Who the hell said you could sleep with my wife?" The man replies, "Everybody!"

•••••

A woman returns home from a business trip. Her little boy greets her at the door saying, "Mommy, guess what? Yesterday I was playing in the closet in your bedroom and Daddy came into the room with the lady next door and they got undressed and got into your bed, and then Daddy got on top of her..." The woman holds up her hand. "Stop, not another word! We'll wait till your father comes home and then I want you to tell him exactly what you've just told me." The man eventually comes home and is confronted by his wife and son. "Go ahead," says the woman. "Tell Daddy what you told me." "Well," says the boy, "I was playing in your bedroom closet and Daddy came upstairs with the lady next door and they got undressed and got into bed, and Daddy got on top of her. And then they did just what you did with Uncle John when Daddy was away last summer!"

• • • • •

Mick's wife is furiously making love with his best friend, Peter, when the phone rings. She hops out of the sweaty bed and, after a brief conversation, she returns. "Who was it?" asks Peter. "Oh, that was Mick," replies the wife. "Shit, I'd better be going!" says Peter. "Relax," replies the wife. "He said he's down at the bar, playing pool with you!"

• • • • •

What did Morris say when he found his best friend in bed with his wife? "Bad dog!"

• • • • •

Zeke walks into the bar. "Hi, Zeke," say his friends. "You put on a great show with your wife last night. You left the light on in your bedroom and we could see everything going on projected on the curtains!" "Sorry, boys," replies Zeke. "The joke's on you—I wasn't home last night!"

• • • • •

Hank calls home one afternoon to see what his wife is making for dinner. "Hello?" says a little girl's voice. "Hi, honey. It's Daddy," says Hank. "Is Mommy near the phone?" "No, Daddy," replies the child. "She's upstairs in the bedroom with Uncle John." Hank says, "But you don't have an Uncle John." "Yes, I do," says the girl. "He's upstairs in the bedroom with Mommy!" "Okay, then," says Hank. "Here's what I want you to do. Put down the phone, knock on the bedroom door, then shout to Mommy and Uncle John that Daddy's car has just pulled up outside the house." A few minutes later, the little girl comes back to the phone. "I did what you said, Daddy. When they heard me, Mommy jumped out of bed and ran around, screaming. Then she tripped over the rug and fell out the window and now she's dead!" "Oh, my God!" says Hank. "And what about Uncle John?" "He jumped out the back window into the swimming pool," replies the girl. "But he must have forgot that you took out all the water last week, so now he's dead, too." There's a long pause, then Hank says, "Swimming pool? Is this 555-7039…?"

Aliens

Mike and Maureen have been kidnapped by aliens. The aliens turn out to be quite friendly, but they want to know how earth people have sex. They decide the easiest way to find out is if Mike has sex with a female alien and Maureen has sex with a male alien. Once this is agreed, Maureen and the male alien go to a bedroom and strip. It turns out the male has a tiny penis about half an inch long and a quarter inch thick. "I don't think this is going to work," says Maureen. "That's not long enough to get inside me." "No problem," replies the alien, and he starts to slap his forehead with his hand. With each slap, his cock grows three inches. The next, the alien starts pulling his ears. With each pull, his cock grows an inch wider. The alien pulls and slaps until his cock gets big enough to satisfy Maureen, then they fall into bed and make mad, passionate love. The next day the aliens drop Mike and Maureen off at their house. Mike says to Maureen, "Well, was it any good?" "I hate to say it," replies Maureen, "but it was pretty fantastic. How about you?" "I had a horrible time," answers Mike,

"All I got was a terrible headache. All night long she was slapping my forehead and pulling my ears..."

Anatomy

A teenage boy asks his father what a lady's "private parts" look like. The father thinks for a moment, then replies, "Well, before sex it sort of looks like a rose with beautiful dark red petals." "Oh, right," says the son. "So does it look any different *after* sex?" "Yes," replies the father. "But it's difficult to describe... Say, have you ever seen a bulldog eating mayonnaise?"

• • • • •

To men it may be an endless source of fascination but you'll never hear a woman say, "My, what an attractive scrotum!"

• • • • •

A woman has very large vaginal lips. She wants them removed so she goes to have corrective surgery. The operation is a success and when the woman wakes up, she finds three bouquets of flowers by her bedside. She asks the doctor who sent them. "Well, one is from me," replies the doctor. "They're a thank-you for being such a good patient. The second bouquet is from your husband to say sorry he wasn't able to be here when you woke up. And the third bouquet is from one of the patients upstairs—he wants to say thanks for his new ears!"

• • • • •

A couple are in bed indulging in foreplay. "Put your finger in me," says the woman. The man does so. "Now put two fingers in me," she moans. He puts in a second finger. "Now stick in your whole hand!" shouts the woman. The man obliges and stuffs his whole hand inside. "Now stick in the other hand!" screams the woman. He does as he's told. The woman screams, "Now clap your hands together!" "I can't!" shouts the guy. The woman looks at him and says, "See, I told you I had a tight pussy!"

• • • • •

What do you call the space between the vagina and the asshole? The chin rest!

• • • • •

A new bride goes to her doctor for a check-up. She has little knowledge of male anatomy, so she asks the doctor a few questions. "Doctor," she says. "What's the name of the thing that hangs between my husband's legs?" He replies, "That's called the penis." The bride then says, "And what's that reddish thing on the end of the penis?" The doctor replies "We call that 'the glans.'" "I see," says the bride. "And what are those two hairy round things about fifteen inches from the tip of the penis?" The doctor replies, "Well, I don't know about your husband, but mine are called butt-cheeks!"

• • • • •

What are the small bumps around women's nipples? It's Braille for "suck here."

•••••

A young woman is about to get married, but is worried that her long history of sexual activity has given her a loose vagina. She tells her mother, who suggests sticking an apple up there. "That'll make it nice and tight," says the mother. "Just make sure your husband doesn't find out." The trick works, but a month after the wedding the daughter runs over to her mother's house and shouts, "Momma, Billy found my apple in the bathroom! I'd taken it out while I was in the shower and he ate the damn thing! Do you think he'll be poisoned?" "Aw, he'll be fine," replies the mother. "Three years ago, your papa ate my watermelon and he's as right as rain!"

•••••

Why is the space between a woman's tits and her hips called a waist? Because you could fit another pair of tits in there!

•••••

Why do women have two holes? So you can carry them like a six-pack when they're drunk!

•••••

An elderly couple, Terry and June, rent a room to a young woman. They don't have a bathroom and the bathing arrangement consists of a tin bath in the parlor. One evening, while Terry is out playing darts at the bar, the lodger takes a bath and June accidentally catches sight of her naked. Later in bed June tells Terry that their lodger has got shaved privates. "Wow!" says Terry. "I wonder what that looks like?" "Tell you what," says June. "When you go to play darts tomorrow I'll leave the curtains open a crack and you can look into the parlor when she's taking her bath." Next evening June leaves the curtains slightly open and stands near the window while the lodger takes her bath. Sure enough the lodger's privates are in full view and, by way of comparison, June lifts her skirts to reveal her own hairiness to Terry, watching outside. Later in bed June asks Terry what he thought of the experience. "It was interesting," says Terry. "But why did you have to lift your skirts like that?" "Well, why not?" asks June. "It's nothing you haven't seen before." "Yeah, I know *I've* seen it before," replies Terry. "But the rest of the darts team hadn't!"

• • • • •

Three old women are sitting in a bar. One boasts, "My pussy is so big my husband can stick his fist up it." The second woman says, "Well, mine is so big my husband can stick his foot in it!" The third woman just laughs and slides down her barstool.

• • • • •

What does a woman do with her asshole while she's having sex? She leaves him at home!

Anniversaries

On their 25th wedding anniversary, a man takes his wife on a trip to the hotel where they spent their honeymoon. They book the same room as on their wedding night and find it's almost exactly as they remembered it. "Oh, dar-ling," says the wife. "Tonight will be exactly the same as our first night of wedded bliss." "Yeah," replies the hus-band, "Except this time it'll be *me* lying on the bed scream-ing, 'It's too big, it's too big...!'"

•••••

A wife approaches her husband wearing the same sexy negligee she wore on their wedding night. "Honey," she says. "Do you remember this? I wore it on our honey-moon." "Yes, I do remember it," he replies. "And do you remember what you said to me that night?" asks his wife. The husband replies, "As I recall, I said, 'Baby, I'm going to suck the life out of those big tits and screw your brains out!'" "That's right," giggles his wife. "And what are you going to say to me tonight?" The husband looks her up and down and says, "Mission accomplished!"

•••••

A couple are celebrating their golden wedding anniver-sary when the husband asks his wife if she's ever been unfaithful. "Three times," she answers. "Remember when you needed money to start up your business and no one would give you any? Well, I screwed the bank manager to secure you a loan." "You made that sacrifice for me?" asks the astonished husband, "Well, that was wonderful. What was the second time?" "Remember that operation you needed and no one would perform it because it was too dangerous?" asks the wife. "Well, I screwed the surgeon so he'd do it." "Oh, my God!" says the husband, "you saved my life. And what was the third time?" "Well," says his wife. "Remember when you wanted to be president of the golf club and you were fifty-two votes short…?"

Anthropology

An anthropologist is visiting an Indian reservation when he notices a chief wearing an unusual bracelet decorated with animal bones. Curious, he asks what it symbolizes. "This humpaa bracelet," replies the chief. "For every humpaa I screw, I get to add bone to bracelet." "I see," says the puzzled anthropologist. "But what exactly is a 'humpaa'?" "Humpaa is everywhere," replies the chief. "Beaver is 'humpaa.' I screw beaver, I add to bracelet. Bear is 'humpaa.' I screw bear, I add to bracelet. Skunk is 'humpaa.' I screw skunk, I add to bracelet…" "Oh, dear," says the embarrassed anthropologist. "No," replies the chief. "*Not* 'humpaa'! Never screw deer— their assholes too high and they run too fast!"

· · · · ·

Two explorers are watching a native ceremony in an African village. Twenty naked men are arranged in a circle facing inward, each faced by a kneeling native woman. "It's a form of Russian roulette," explains one of the explorers. "When the chief bangs the drum, the men move to their left. When the banging ceases, the men stop. Each woman then gives the man in front of her a blow job." "That doesn't sound as risky as Russian roulette," comments the other explorer. "Oh, it is," says the first explorer. "You see, one of the girls is a cannibal!"

Art

At an art exhibition a woman is looking at a portrait of three naked black men sitting on a bench. Two of the men have black penises, but the one in the middle has a pink penis. The curator of the gallery stops by and offers his assessment of this curious imagery. He goes on for half an hour, explaining how it depicts the sexual emasculation of black men in a predominately white, patriarchal society. After the curator leaves an old man approaches the woman and says, "I'm the one who painted that picture. Would you like to know what it's *really* about?" "Okay," replies the woman. "So what is it about?" "They're three coal miners," says the old man. "And the one in the middle went home for his lunch!"

Asians

A waitress in a restaurant notices three Japanese business-men sitting at a table masturbating furiously. "What the hell are you guys doing?" she asks. "I'm so sorry," says one of the men. "But we very, very hungry... We been waiting here for one hour." "But what's that go to do with you three jerking off?" asks the waitress. The man replies, "Menu say 'first come, first served'!"

•••••

A woman goes to a Chinese sex therapist named Dr. Chang to see if he can solve her difficulty in finding sex partners. Dr. Chang says, "Take off all yo' clothes and crawl real fass away from me across the froor." She does so and crawls to the other side of the room. Dr. Chang then says, "Now yo' crawl real fass back to me." She does this, too. Dr. Chang shakes his head and says, "You haf real bad case of Ed Zachary syndrome. Worse case I ever seen! No wonder you can never get date." The woman is baffled. "So what the heck is Ed Zachary syndrome?" she asks. Dr. Chang replies, "You must 'a heard of Ed Zachary Syndrome—that's when your face look Ed Zachary rike your ass!"

•••••

A young man is wandering through China when he comes upon a house in the mountains. He knocks on the door and is greeted by an ancient Chinese man. "I'm lost," says the young man. "Can you put me up for the night?" "Certainly," the old man replies. "But on one condition... If you so much as lay a finger on my young daughter I will inflict upon you the three worst Chinese tortures known to man." The man agrees and is invited to sit at the dinner table. But the old man's daughter turns out to be young and beautiful and later on, the man creeps into her room for a night of passion. At dawn, he creeps back to his room, exhausted, and goes to sleep. A little while later he wakes to feel something pressing on him. He opens his eyes and sees a large rock on his chest with a note reading, "Chinese Torture 1: Large rock on chest." "That's pretty crappy," thinks the man. "If that's the best he can do, I don't have much to worry about." The man gets up, walks to the window and throws the boulder out into a deep ravine. As he does so, he notices another note stuck to the window frame. It reads, "Chinese Torture 2: Rock tied to left testicle." The man looks down and sees that his testicle is indeed tied to the falling rock. The man jumps out the window, hoping for a soft landing that will save his testicle. Suddenly he sees a third note pinned to the rope. As he falls, he reads, "Chinese Torture 3: Right testicle tied to bedpost."

•••••

An American businessman is out in Japan, visiting clients. One evening he goes to the local red light district and picks up a prostitute. He takes her back to his hotel and they jump into bed. The man starts screwing like crazy and the prostitute keeps shouting, "Yagazaki! Yagazaki...!" Assuming this is a compliment, he proceeds to screw her even harder. The next day he's out playing golf with some of his clients. One of the Japanese men gets a hole in one and the businessman shows his appreciation by shouting, "Yagazaki!" The Japanese man looks at him and asks, "What do you mean 'wrong hole'?"

•••••

Bill calls his local Chinese restaurant and asks, "Is Haf-In there?" "Sorry," replies the man on the phone. "He not here." "Then can I speak to Haf-Out?" asks Bill. "Sorry," the man replies. "He not here either." "Who am I speaking to?" asks Bill. The man replies, "Me Haf-Up, the cook." "Sorry," says Bill. "I'll call back when you're not so busy!"

Australians

Two Aussies, Liam and Aaron, are adrift in a lifeboat when they see a lamp. Liam rubs it and a genie appears saying he'll grant one wish. Liam yells, "Turn the ocean into Fosters!" The genie nods and the sea turns into beer. Aaron says, "Nice going mate! Now we'll have to pee in the boat."

•••••

A middle-aged spinster wants to get married but will only consider a gentleman who's never made love to a woman. A man like this proves hard to find, but eventually she tracks down a willing partner—a gold prospector who's lived all his life isolated in the Australian outback. They get married, but on their wedding night the woman is surprised to find her husband standing naked in the living room. What's more, the carpets have been rolled back and the furniture is piled in the corner. "What are you doing?" asks the woman. "Well, I've never made love to a woman," replies her husband. "But if it's anything like fucking a kangaroo, I'm going to need all the room I can get!"

•••••

A tourist is driving through the Australian bush when he sees a man having sex with a kangaroo. Appalled, he heads back toward town to report this incident, but as he drives he's shocked to see another man having sex with a kangaroo, and then another. Disgusted, he drives into town only to see a man with a wooden leg masturbating outside a bar. The tourist pulls up outside the police station and accosts the sergeant. "I was out in the bush when I saw three men having sex with kangaroos!" "Did you really?" asks the sergeant. "Yes," replies the tourist. "And then I saw a man with a wooden leg masturbating in the street. How can you tolerate such dirty behavior?" "Well, be fair, mate," replies the sergeant, "How's the poor bastard going to catch a kangaroo in his condition?"

Batteries

A woman goes into a shop and asks if they have batteries. "Yes, ma'am," says the shop assistant, gesturing with his finger. "Can you come this way?" The woman replies, "If I could come *that* way, I wouldn't need the batteries!"

Bikers

A motorcycle cop comes across two bikers. One biker has his index finger up the backside of the other. "What the heck are you doing?" asks the cop. "My buddy here is choking," replies the biker with the finger. "I'm trying to get him to throw up." "You're supposed to stick your finger down his throat, not up his backside," says the cop. The biker replies, "Yeah, but you get better results if you stick it up his ass first!"

•••••

A doctor, an accountant and a biker are discussing anniversary presents. The doctor says, "I bought my wife a diamond ring and a new car. I figured if she didn't like the ring, she'd love the car." The accountant says, "I bought my wife a pendant and a speedboat. I figured if she didn't like the pendant, she'd love the speedboat." The biker says, "I bought my chick a T-shirt and a dildo. I figured if she didn't like the T-shirt, she could go fuck herself!"

• • • • •

An elderly woman decides she needs protection in her old age and figures the best way to get it is to join a gang. She hobbles over to the local Hell's Angels club and taps on the door. "Excuse me, gentlemen, I'd like to join your gang," she croaks. A bearded biker sneers at her, "You got no chance, woman. We take only the toughest into our gang—you can only join if you drink!" "Well, I *do* drink!" she replies. "I'm very fond of sherry." "Okay," says the biker, "But we'll only take you if you do drugs as well." "Oh, I do drugs," she says. "I'm on fifteen prescriptions." "Yeah?" says the biker. "Well, we only want mean law-breakers in our gang. Have you ever been picked up by the fuzz?" "Well, no," says the old lady, "but I have been swung around by the tits a few times!"

Blondes

Did you hear about the new blonde paint? It's not very bright, but it's cheap and spreads easy.

How can you tell if a blonde has been using your Playstation? The joystick is wet.

How can you tell if a blonde's been in your refrigerator? There's lipstick on your cucumbers.

How can you tell when a blonde is having her period? She's only wearing one sock.

How do you describe the perfect blonde? Three feet tall, no teeth and a flat head to rest your beer on!

How do you know if a blonde has just lost her virginity? Her crayons are still sticky.

How can you tell if a blonde did your landscaping? The bushes are darker than the rest of the yard.

How does a blonde answer the question, "Are you sexually active?" She says, "No, I just lie there."

How does a blonde hold her liquor? By the ears!

How does a blonde part her hair? She does the splits.

How would a blonde punctuate the following, "Fun, fun, fun, worry, worry, worry...?" "Fun, period, fun, period, fun, no period, worry, worry, worry!"

Most men regard blondes as a golden opportunity.

What did the blonde's left leg say to her right leg? "Between the two of us, we can make a lot of money."

What did the blonde's mother say to her before her date? "If you're not in bed by 12, come home!"

What did the blonde's right leg say to the left leg? Nothing, they've never met!

What do a bleached blonde and a jumbo jet have in common? They both have a black box.

What do a blonde and a turtle have in common? Get 'em on their back and they're both fucked!

What do blondes put behind their ears to attract men? Their knees!

What do blondes shout after multiple orgasms? "Way to go, team!"

What do the Bermuda Triangle and a blonde have in common? They've both swallowed a lot of semen.

What do you call a blonde with a runny nose? Full!

What do you call a blonde with ESP and PMS? A know-it-all bitch.

What do you call a blonde with pigtails? A blow job with handlebars.

What do you call a brunette and three blondes on a corner? You don't—you check to see if you've got three condoms.

What does a blonde look like after sex? No one stays around long enough to find out.

What does a blonde say after having sex? Which team do you guys play for?

What do a screen door and a blonde have in common? The more you bang it, the looser it gets!

What's the difference between a blond guy and a blonde girl? The blonde girl's sperm count is higher.

What's the difference between a blonde and a 747? Not everyone's been in a 747.

What's the difference between a blonde and a broom closet? Only two men fit inside a broom closet at once.

What's the difference between a blonde and a mosquito? When you smack the mosquito, it stops sucking.

What's the difference between a blonde and a pair of sunglasses? The glasses sit higher on your face.

What's the difference between a blonde and a phone booth? You need a quarter to use the phone.

What's the difference between a blonde and an inflatable doll? About two cans of hair spray.

What's the difference between a blonde and an ironing board? It's difficult to open the legs on an ironing board.

What's the difference between a corn farmer with epilepsy and a blonde with diarrhea? One shucks between fits.

What's the difference between a prostitute, a nymphomaniac and a blonde? The prostitute asks, "Aren't you done yet?" The nympho asks, "Are you done already?" But the blonde says, "Beige, I think I'll paint the ceiling beige…"

What's the difference between a walrus and a blonde? One is wet, has a moustache and smells of fish. The other is a walrus!

What's the difference between butter and a blonde? Butter is hard to spread.

What's the first thing a blonde does in the morning? Introduces herself, then walks home.

What's the mating call of the blonde? "I'm so drunk!" What's the mating call of the ugly blonde? "I said, 'I'm sooo drunk!'"

What's the quickest way to get into a blonde's pants? Pick them up off the floor.

Why are blondes like dog turds? The older they get, the easier they are to pick up.

Why can't blondes count to 70? Because 69 is too much of a mouthful.

Why can't blondes pass their driving tests? Whenever the car stops, they hop in the back seat.

Why can't blondes waterski? Once they get their crotch wet, they think they have to lie down.

Why did the blonde insist on her boyfriend wearing a condom? So she could have a doggie bag for later.

Why did the blonde like the car with a sunroof? More leg room!

Why did the deaf blonde sit on the newspaper? So she could lip-read.

Why do blondes have bruised belly buttons? Because they have blond boyfriends.

Why do blondes have more fun? They're easier to find in the dark.

Why do blondes like tilt steering wheels? More headroom.

Why do blondes wear hoop earrings? So they have a place to rest their ankles.

Why do blondes wear underwear? To keep their ankles warm.

Why don't blondes eat dill pickles? Because they can't get their heads in the jar.

Why don't blondes use vibrators? They chip their teeth.

Why is a blonde like a doorknob? Because everyone gets a turn.

Why is a blonde like a halogen headlight? They both get screwed on the front of a car.

Why is a blonde like an old washing machine? Because they both drip when they're fucked!

Why was the blonde upset when she got her driver's license? She only got an "F" in sex.

Blow Jobs

Bill, to Jeff, "Did I tell you about the worst blow job I ever got?" Jeff, "No, I don't think you did." Bill, "It was great!"

•••••

A little boy gets up to go to the bathroom in the middle of the night. As he passes his parents' bedroom he peeks in through the keyhole. He watches for a moment, then continues on down the hallway, saying to himself, "Boy, and she gets mad at me for sucking my thumb!"

•••••

What's the best thing about a blow job? The five minutes of silence.

•••••

How do you know you've had a good blow job? When you have to pull six inches of bed sheets out of your ass!

•••••

A young man, Bill, drops off his girlfriend at her home. They reach the front door and Bill leans casually on the doorframe. "So," he asks. "How about you giving me a blow job?" "What?" the girl replies. "Are you crazy?" "Don't worry, it'll be quick," he says. "No," she says. "Someone might see us." "It's just a blow job," insists Bill. "You might like it—and you don't have to swallow if you don't want to." "No," says the girl. "Don't be disgusting." "Aww, come on," whines Bill. "Just take it in your hand…" At that moment the front door opens. It's the girl's mother. "Honey," she says. "Either blow him, or tell him to get lost; either way Daddy wants him to take his hand off the intercom!"

•••••

A man goes to his dentist for a checkup. The dentist looks in his mouth and comments: "I see you had oral sex this morning." "Christ, you're right!" says the man. "How can you tell? Did you see a pubic hair in my teeth?" "No," replies the dentist. "But the dab of shit on your nose is a dead giveaway!"

•••••

How do you get a woman to stop giving you oral sex? Marry her!

Breasts

A woman with a flat chest goes shopping for a new bra. She goes into shop after shop, asking if they have a size 28A, but she can't find one anywhere. Eventually she tries her luck in a small lingerie shop run by an old, deaf lady. "Have you got anything in size 28A?" asks the woman. "What was that, dear?" replies the old lady. The woman lifts up her T-shirt to expose her breasts and shouts, "Have you got anything for these?" The old lady peers at the woman's boobs and replies, "No, dear. Have you tried acne cream?"

•••••

How is the WonderBra like a cattle drive? They both head 'em up and move 'em out!

•••••

I'm going to tell you a joke that's so funny you'll laugh your tits off. Oops, you've already heard it.

•••••

What did the bra say to the hat? You go on ahead and I'll give these two a lift!

•••••

What happened to the large-breasted streaker at the rock concert? She was thrown out by the bouncers!

•••••

Why is the WonderBra called a WonderBra? Because when she takes it off, you wonder where her goddamn breasts went!

•••••

A guy walks into a psychiatrist's office complaining of trouble with women. The shrink asks him what he looks for in a woman, and he replies, "Big tits." "No," says the shrink. "I mean for a serious relationship." "Oh," says the guy. "Sorry. In that case it's seriously big tits." "No, no, no," says the shrink. "I mean, what do you look for in the woman you want to spend the rest of your life with?" And the guy sits there on the couch laughing hysterically. "Spend the rest of my life with one woman? Are you kidding? No one's got tits that big!"

•••••

This guy is walking down the street when he sees a gorgeous blonde woman with perfect mouth-watering tits. He goes up to her and says, "Hey, I'll give you $10 to let me bite your tits." She replies in disgust, "Are you crazy? No!" The guy sighs and then says, "Okay. I'll give you $100 dollars to let me bite your tits." And the girl still says, "No way!" So the guy sighs again and says, " Okay. I'll give you $1,000 to let me bite your tits." The girl hesitates, but still replies, "No." Finally, the guy says, "All right. I'll give you $10,000 to let me bite your tits." This time, the girl replies, "Wow! Ten thousand? Okay!" So they go into an alleyway where the beautiful blonde lifts off her shirt and bra. The guy begins to fondle her tits and rub them against himself. After a few minutes of this, the girl asks, "So are you gonna bite them yet or what?" And the guy replies, "Are you kidding? For ten thousand dollars? I can't afford that!"

Camels

A man buys a camel from a zoo and rides it into the parking lot of his local bar. "Nice camel," says one of his drinking friends. "Is it male or female?" "Female!" replies the man. "How do you know?" asks his friend. "It has to be," replies the man. "On the way here, at least twenty people shouted, 'Hey, look at the cunt on that camel!'"

•••••

A man is riding through the desert on a camel. After many months alone he gets so horny, he decides to have sex with the beast. Unfortunately, there's nothing to tie the camel to, and as soon as he tries to position the animal for sex it runs away. The man tries again and again, but the camel keeps running away. Eventually the man catches up with the camel by a broken-down car. Sitting in the car are three beautiful blondes. He goes over to see if they need help. "Our car won't start," says one of the blondes. "If you fix it we'll be *ever* so grateful—we'll do *anything* you want." The man fixes the car in a flash, then goes to claim his reward. "So what can we do for you, handsome?" pouts one of the girls. "Miss, you and your friends are exactly what I need," the man responds. "Can you hold my camel for me...?"

•••••

There's a new commander at the Foreign Legion fort. The captain is showing him around when the commander spots a small blue hut. "What's in there?" he asks. The captain replies, "It's where we keep the camel. There are no women here, so whenever the men feel the need for female company, they use the camel." The commander is disgusted by this idea, but after six months of celibacy he decides to give it a try. He goes to the captain, gets the key to the blue hut and sneaks over to it. On opening the hut door, the commander finds the camel with its back to him so he climbs on a stool, drops his pants and starts to have sex with it. After a few minutes the commander realizes the captain is standing behind him holding a saddle. "Begging your pardon, sir," says the captain, "But I thought you might like to borrow my saddle. You see, if the men want a woman they usually ride the camel into town!"

•••••

Pierre joins the Foreign Legion and is posted to a remote desert fort. The sergeant explains to him that the men rely on camels for sex and that evening a whole herd are released in the grounds of the fort. The men go wild, chasing camels all over the place, desperate to have their wicked way. Pierre loiters by the gate, watching the goings-on with disgust. The sergeant sees him and shouts, "Hey!

What are you waiting for?" "What's the hurry?" replies Pierre. "There must be over a hundred camels here." "Suit yourself," says the sergeant. "But don't blame me if you get stuck with an ugly one!"

• • • • •

What's Osama Bin Laden's idea of safe sex? Marking the camels that kick!

Cannibals

What's the true definition of trust? Two cannibals having oral sex.

• • • • •

Two starving cannibals capture a missionary. To divide him equally they agree to start eating him from opposite ends and make their way to the middle. After five minutes of munching, one says, "How are you doing down there?" The other replies, "I'm having a ball." "Then slow down!" replies the first. "You're eating too fast!"

• • • • •

What did Jeffrey Dahmer say to Lorena Bobbitt? "Are you going to eat that?"

• • • • •

What did the cannibal do after he dumped his girlfriend? Wiped his ass!

Cars

A man is in the back of his car having sex with a woman he picked up in a bar. The woman is insatiable and keeps demanding more. Finally, the man takes a break and steps out for a smoke. Once out of the car he notices a man nearby, changing the tire on his pick-up truck. The first man goes over and says, "Look, I've got a really hot date in that car and I can't keep up with her. If I change your tire, will you get in there and have sex with her? It's pitch black, so she won't know the difference." The second man agrees and jumps into the back of the car, which soon starts to rock rhythmically. A passing policeman notices this activity and shines a flashlight in the back of the car. "What's going on in there?" he asks. The man replies, "I'm having sex with my wife." "Why can't you do that at home?" asks the policeman. The man replies, "Because I didn't realize it was my wife till you shined that flashlight in her face!"

•••••

Around midnight a cop sees a car weaving on the road and pulls it over. At the wheel is a young woman, who reeks of whisky. "I'm going to have to give you a breathalyzer test, ma'am," says the cop, and gets her to blow in the bag. He looks at the indicator strip and says, "Yup, looks like you've had three or four stiff ones tonight." "Oh, my God," slurs the woman. "You mean it shows that, too?"

•••••

Jake is driving around town in a Rolls-Royce when he sees his friend Gary. He pulls over to say hello. "How did you get the car?" asks Gary. "Well," says Jake. "I was walking down the street when the gorgeous woman pulled up in this car and offered me a ride. I got in and she asked me to kiss her, so I did. Then she parked up a lane and took off all her clothes except her silk panties. Then she lay back in her seat and said, 'Take anything you want from me.'" "Wow!" says Gary. "What did you do then?" "Well," replies Jake. "I could see her underwear would never fit me, so I took the car."

Celebrations

A man is drinking champagne in a bar when he sees a woman doing the same. "Are you celebrating?" he asks. "Yes," replies the woman. "After years of infertility my doctor has just told me I'm pregnant." "That's great," says the man. "I'm celebrating, too. I'm a chicken farmer and for months my hens haven't been laying. I solved the problem and now they're laying eggs like crazy." "How did you do that?" asks the woman. "I changed cocks," replies the man. "Same here," replies the woman.

• • • • •

A man walks into a bar and orders nine double martinis to be put on a line on the bar top. The bartender lines up the drinks and watches as the man knocks them back one after the other. "Why all the drinks?" he asks. "I'm celebrating my first blow job," the man replies. "Congratulations," says the bartender. "Let me give you one on the house to make it an even ten." "No, thanks," the man replies. "If nine won't get the taste out of my mouth, one more won't help!"

•••••

Two women go for a girls' night on the town and get very drunk. Staggering home they become desperate for a piss and duck into a cemetery. When they've finished, the first woman uses her panties to wipe herself, then throws them away. The other woman is wearing expensive underwear, so she wipes herself with a card from a nearby wreath. The following morning the two husbands are comparing notes over the phone. One says, "I think we need to start keeping a closer eye on our wives. My wife came home without any underwear on." The other replies, "Tell me about it: My wife came home with a card stuck to her pussy that read, 'We will never forget you.'"

Celebs

How can you recognize Dolly Parton's kids? They have stretchmarks around their lips!

What are pink and fluffy, and never move? Stephen Hawking's slippers.

What do you call a Beatle with wings? John Lennon.

What was the name of Elton John's tribute song to Mother Teresa? "Sandals in the Bin."

Which recording artist had five consecutive hits in one day? John Lennon.

Circumcision

Why are Jewish men circumcised? Because Jewish women won't touch anything unless it's 20% off!

•••••

After a long career as a circumcision specialist a surgeon retires. Throughout his career he's saved hundreds of foreskins as mementos and now wants to turn them into a souvenir. He takes his specimens to a leatherworker and asks him to make something out of them. A week later the surgeon returns and the man gives him a wallet. "All those foreskins and you only made me one lousy wallet!" exclaims the surgeon. The leatherworker replies, "Yeah, but if you stroke it, it turns into a briefcase!"

•••••

Two five-year-old boys are standing at a urinal. One remarks, "Your thingy doesn't have any skin on it!" "I've been circumcised," the other explains. "That means they cut the skin off the end." "Wow!" exclaims the first boy. "When did that happen?" "When I was two days old," the second boy replies. "Did it hurt?" asks the first boy. "Holy crap, you bet it did!" he replies. "I didn't walk for a year!"

•••••

What happened to the short-sighted circumciser? He got the sack!

• • • • •

Ladies, what's the difference between getting a divorce and getting circumcised? When you get a divorce, you get rid of the whole prick!

Clocks

A man walks into a shop selling watches and clocks. He unzips his pants and slaps his cock on the counter. The woman behind the counter doesn't bat an eyelid. She looks him straight in the eye and says, "Put that away, sir. This is a *clock* shop, not a *cock* shop!" "Well," the man replies, "Why don't you put two hands and a face on it?"

Coming of Age

A young boy rushes home and says to his father, "Dad! Dad! You'll never guess what? I had sex with the English teacher!" The father is delighted. "You young scamp," he says. "You're just like me—a real ladies' man. Tell you what, now you're so grown up, I think we can let you ride your big brother's motorbike." The boy's face drops, "Aww, I can't," he whines. "My ass still hurts!"

• • • • •

One day Little Susie gets her period for the first time. Not certain what's happening, she decides to tell Little Johnny. Little Susie lifts her skirt and shows Little Johnny what's happening. His eyes open wide. "You know," he says. "I'm no doctor, but it looks like someone just ripped your balls off!"

•••••

A boy has prudish parents who are very strict and never allow him to interact with girls. One day the boy sees his best friend kissing a girl and asks his mother what they're doing. Mother says, "It's called kissing and any boy who does that to a girl will die in a minute!" Years later, on his 21st birthday, the boy goes out with some friends who introduce him to the sexiest girl in town. The girl knows he's never been kissed, so she gets him alone and tries to give him a smacker. "No!" cries the boy. "My mother told me I'd die in a minute if I did that!" "Don't be a baby," says the girl. "It won't hurt." And she gives him a kiss square on the lips. The boy begins to cry, "Oh, no, I'm dying! You only gave me one and already part of me has begun to get stiff!"

•••••

When does a Cub become a Boy Scout? When he eats his first Brownie.

Competition

A man and woman get into an argument about who enjoys sex the most, males or females. The man says, "Men obviously enjoy sex more than women. Why do you think we're so obsessed with getting laid?" "That doesn't prove anything," replies the woman. "Think about this: When your ear itches and you put your finger in it and wiggle it around, which feels better—your ear or your finger?"

•••••

A woman goes on a quiz show and does very well. In fact she's invited back the next day to compete for the million dollar prize. That night the woman's husband sneaks into the studio and steals the answer to the million dollar question. "Listen," he tells her. "When they ask the question, all you have to do is repeat, 'Head, heart and penis.'" The wife commits this to memory, but on the day she's so nervous, her memory starts to fail her. The time arrives and the quiz host asks her the million dollar question, "According to tradition, which are the three main organs of the male body?" "Oh, dear," says the woman. "It was the, er... the head. The um... the heart... And, er..." "Ten seconds to go," says the host. "Oh, dear," says the woman. "What was it? All last night my husband kept drilling it into me and this morning I had it on the tip of my tongue..." "Close enough!" shouts the host. "You've just won a million dollars!"

•••••

Leroy and Jeff decide to have a competition to see who can have the most sex in an evening. They go to a whorehouse and take the ladies of their choice to their rooms. Jeff energetically screws his partner and makes a mark on the wall to keep score. After a short rest he has sex again and makes another mark. A little while later he does it again and makes another mark, then falls fast asleep. The next morning Leroy knocks on Jeff's door. "How did you do?" he asks. "Oh, pretty good," replies Jeff. "I'm hot stuff."

Leroy sees the three marks on the wall. "Holy crap! You *are* hot! One hundred and eleven! Dammit, you beat me by three."

• • • • •

Mrs. Cohen, Mrs. Levy and Mrs. Lefkovitz are discussing their sons. Mrs. Cohen boasts, "My Sheldon is a world-famous lawyer with big-shot clients, a mansion in Beverly Hills and a summer home in Hawaii. He has a beautiful wife and everything a man could want." Mrs. Levy says, "That's nice. But let me tell you about my son Jonathan. He's a doctor, a world-famous researcher. He was nominated for a Nobel Prize in medicine." Mrs. Lefkowitz responds, "Well, my Hershel might not be rich or famous, but his pee-pee is so long, ten pigeons can perch on it in a line." The ladies pause for thought. Mrs. Cohen says, "Actually, I got a confession to make: Sheldon's an up-and-coming lawyer in Los Angeles, but he doesn't have a mansion or a summer home." Mrs. Levy says, "I've got a confession, too. Jonathan is a good doctor but he never won a Nobel Prize." Mrs. Cohen and Mrs. Levy look expectantly at Mrs. Lefkowitz. "Well, all right," admits Mrs. Lefkowitz. "The last pigeon has to stand on one leg!"

• • • • •

Patrick and Michael go to a bar and see a sign saying, "Buy a double whisky and get a chance of free sex." They both buy a double and ask the bartender how to get the sex. "It's simple," he says. "I think of a number between one and ten, and if you can guess what it is, you get laid." "Okay," says Patrick. "I'll guess, three." "Sorry," the bartender replies. "You're out of luck." The next day the pair return and again, Patrick tries his luck at the free sex quiz. This time he guesses four. "Sorry," says the bartender. "Better luck next time." The next day they return. This time Patrick guesses two. "Sorry," says the bartender. "Wrong again." Patrick turns to Michael and says, "You know I'm beginning to think this contest is rigged." "Oh, no," Michael replies. "My wife tried it last week and she won three times!"

• • • • •

The U.S. Navy decides to offer an early retirement bonus for its officers. Any officer who volunteers for retirement will get a bonus of $1,000 for every inch measured in a straight line between any two parts of their body. One officer accepts the deal and asks to be measured from his head to his feet. This comes to six feet and the officer receives a bonus of $72,000. A second officer asks to be measured from the tip of his outstretched hands to the end of his toes. He walks out with $96,000. Then a third officer asks to be measured from the tip of his penis to the bottom of his testicles. A doctor is summoned and the officer drops his pants. "Okay," says doctor. "I've got the ruler. Here's your penis and … what! Where the hell are your testicles?" The officer replies, "In Vietnam!"

• • • • •

Three men are stranded on a desert island and are captured by cannibals. The cannibals take the men back to their village, where they're told that the cannibal chief has the longest penis on the island. If the combined lengths of the men's penises beat the chief, the men can go free; otherwise they'll be eaten. The chief lifts his grass skirt and the men are horrified to see that the chief's penis must be at least twenty inches long. The first man drops his pants and his penis is measured at ten inches. Then the second man is measured at nine inches. The third man drops his pants and he's measured at one inch. Since the final tally equals the chief, they're allowed to go. The first man breathes a sigh of relief, "Good thing for us I had a ten-inch penis," he says. "Well, it was a good thing I had a nine-inch penis," the second man replies. The third man remarks, "It was a good thing I had an erection!"

• • • • •

Two cowboys are talking in a bar. The conversation turns to sex and the first cowboy says, "Say, have you ever heard of the Rodeo Position?" "No," replies his friend. "How does that work?" "It's a lot of fun," replies the first cowboy. "You mount your wife from behind, grab her tits and say, 'Hey, these are almost as good as your sister's!' Then you see if you can stay on for more than eight seconds!"

Condoms and Contraception

A woman is asked how she feels about condoms. She says, "Dunno, depends on what's in it for me!"

• • • • •

Why do condoms have a bubble on the end? To put your foot on when you're taking it off!

• • • • •

A man goes into a drugstore to buy some condoms. He sees a new brand on sale for half-price but isn't sure of the size he needs, so he asks the girl behind the counter for some help. "How big are you?" she asks. "Compared to what?" the man replies. "Are you *that* big?" asks the girl, holding up one finger. "I'm bigger than that," replies the man. The girl holds up two fingers. "Are you as big as *that*?" she asks. "Yes," replies the man. The girl then holds up three fingers. "So, are you *that* big?" she asks. The man looks at the fingers and says, "Well, yes. I guess I am." The girl sticks the three fingers in her mouth, wiggles them around a bit and then takes them out again. "That makes you a medium," she says.

• • • • •

Guys, don't buy expensive "ribbed" condoms, buy ordinary ones and throw in some frozen peas!

• • • • •

A man with a nervous tick applies for a job in a store. Unfortunately, his tick makes it look as though he's winking all the time and it starts to put customers off. The store manager calls him over and explains the situation. "It's not a problem," says the man. "I forgot to take my aspirin. All I need is a couple of pills and the winking will stop for the day." So, he reaches into his pockets to find some aspirin and starts dragging out handfuls of condoms. "Why all the condoms?" asks the manager. "You're not some sort of sex maniac, are you?" "No," replies the man, "But they're what you get if you walk into a drugstore winking and ask for a pack of aspirins!"

•••••

Why did the Irishman wear two condoms? To be sure, to be sure.

•••••

Why did the condom cross the road? Because it was pissed off!

•••••

A woman is smoking a cigarette at a bus stop when it starts to rain. A man is doing the same and when he feels the first drop of rain, he takes a condom out of his pocket, tears the end off and slips it over his cigarette to keep it dry. "What a great idea," thinks the woman and hurries over to a drugstore. "Can I have a packet of condoms?" she asks the salesclerk. "Certainly, madam," he replies. "What size?" The woman replies, "One that will fit a Camel!"

•••••

Why should you wear ribbed condoms for anal sex? Better traction in the mud!

•••••

What do a camera and a condom have in common? They both capture that magic moment.

•••••

A woman phones her doctor in the middle of the night, saying, "Doctor, come quick. My son has just swallowed a condom!" The doctor gets out of bed and is hurriedly putting on his clothes when the phone rings again. It's the same woman. "It's alright," she says. "You don't have to come out after all—my husband's just found another one!"

•••••

An elderly couple go to a drugstore to buy a packet of condoms. "Do you mind me asking how old you are?" asks the salesclerk. "I'm 75," the old man replies. "And my wife is 73." "Well, in that case you don't need condoms," replies the clerk. "It's very unlikely that your wife will conceive at that age." "Oh, we don't want them for that," replies the old man. "It's for my wife—she loves the smell of burning rubber!"

•••••

Did you hear about the new "morning after" pill for men? It changes their blood type.

•••••

Do you know how to reuse a condom? Turn it inside out and wash the fuck out of it!

•••••

One day a husband is out shopping when he notices a new brand of condoms called "Olympic." He buys a pack and shows his wife. "Olympic condoms?" she asks. "What's so special about them?" "They come in three different colors," replies the husband. "Gold, Silver and Bronze!" "So what color are you going to wear tonight?" asks the wife. "Gold, of course!" he replies. "Really?" asks his wife, "Why don't you try Silver? It would be nice if you came second for a change!"

•••••

Practice safe sex… Go screw yourself!

•••••

The sergeant major of a Scottish Regiment goes into a drugstore and places a tattered old condom on the counter. "How much to repair that?" he asks. "Oh, dear," replies the clerk. "It's in bad shape. I can sew it up there, and glue it here and here, but it'll need tape down the edges and a very thorough wash. To be honest, it might be better to buy a new one." The sergeant major promises to think about it. The next day he returns and says, "I'll take one of your condoms, please. I had a word with the boys and they reckon a new one would be a good investment!"

•••••

My wife's got her very own method of birth control—she takes off her make-up!

•••••

A young couple have just had sex. The woman asks, "If I get pregnant, what shall we call the baby?" The man takes off his condom, ties a knot in it and flushes it down the toilet. "Well," he replies. "If he can get out of that, we'd better call him 'Houdini'!"

Condoms: Uses for Old Ones

A muzzle for a Chihuahua.
A punch bag for a gerbil.
A Christmas stocking for when coal isn't enough to tell
    them how badly they screwed up this year.

Attach them to your nipples and see if you can revolve them in opposite directions to one another.

Break out your paints and make wax fruit.

Drain plugs.

Ear and/or nose plugs.

Enclose them with your tax returns.

Finger puppets.

Freeze them for an all-natural popsicle.

French tickler animals.

Glue a few together and tell your kids it's the new Stretch Armstrong.

Handle grips for your bicycle.

Hang them on the blades of your ceiling fan.

If you have enough, glue them together and use them to replace silicon breast implants.

Jelly moulds.

Little water wings for non-swimmers.

Make your own "water" bed.

Novelty key rings.

Pull four over your cat's feet. That should stop the bastard from scratching the furniture!

Put them on your fingers and let's play proctologist.

Place one over the showerhead to surprise Dad!

Put your money in one—who's going to steal it now?

Recycle as a Burger King ketchup packet (or would mayonnaise be better?).

Replace those old "Dr. Scholls" shoe cushions.

Send fifty of them to your ex-girlfriend.

Slap someone across the face, saying, "I challenge you to a duel!"

Stick one on the bridge of your nose and run around the office saying, "Gobble gobble."

Stretch one over the top of an open can of soda to keep the fizz in.

Surprise Dad again by stretching one over the end of his exhaust pipe!

Swimming caps for the kids.

Use five hundred of them to spell out the message, "We Want Women!" on your roof.

Cosmetic Surgery

A woman suggests to her husband that she have surgery to make her breasts bigger. As an alternative, her husband suggests she rub toilet paper between them. "How would that make my breasts bigger?" she asks. "I don't know," he replies. "But it worked for your goddamn ass!"

•••••

A woman with bags under her eyes goes to see a plastic surgeon, who tries a new technique: He removes the bags, then puts a crank in the back of the woman's head and tells her to turn it if she spots new bags forming. For many years the technique works and then a huge pair of bags appears. No matter how far the woman turns the crank, they refuse to budge. The surgeon examines her and remarks, "No wonder you can't get rid of them—these are your breasts! You've been turning that crank too much." "Oh, I see," says the woman. "And I suppose that would also explain the goatee!"

• • • • •

What's worse than a woman with silicone tits? A woman with a cardboard box!

Cowboys and Indians

A woman from New York is driving through a remote part of Texas when her car breaks down. An Indian on horseback comes along and offers her a ride. She climbs up behind him and they ride off. The trip is uneventful except that every few minutes the Indian lets out a loud whoop. When they arrive in town, the Indian lets her off at the gas station, yells one final, "Yahoo!" and rides off. "What did you do to get that Indian so excited?" asks the gas station attendant. "Nothing," shrugs the woman. "I just sat behind him, put my arms around his waist and held onto his saddle horn to keep me steady." "That'll explain it," says the attendant. "That Indian was riding bareback!"

• • • • •

Some Indians capture a cowboy and decide to put him to death. The Indian chief explains that a custom of the tribe is for a condemned man to be given three wishes. The cowboy asks to see his horse and the horse is brought to him. He then whispers in the horse's ear and the horse runs off. A little while later the horse returns with a naked redhead on its back. The cowboy looks cross, but he and the redhead go into a tepee for half an hour. The Indians watch this activity with contempt. "Typical white man behavior," they mutter to each other. "Is sex all he can think of at a time like this?" Once the cowboy and the redhead have finished, the cowboy asks for his second wish: to see his horse once more. The horse is brought over and again, the cowboy whispers in its ear. The horse runs off and returns an hour later with a naked blonde on its back. Again, the cowboy looks cross, but he and the blonde retire to his wigwam. Once more the Indians mutter about the depravity of the white man. After an hour the cowboy comes out of the wigwam and requests his last wish: He wants to see his horse again. The horse is led to him, the cowboy whispers in its ear and the horse runs off. After three hours the horse returns with a naked brunette on its back. The Indians are astonished. "What's with this guy?" they murmur. "Is he some sort of sex maniac?" The cowboy is furious. He walks over to the horse and shouts, "Are you fucking deaf? I said 'posse'!"

•••••

The Lone Ranger and Tonto are out in the desert when the Lone Ranger asks Tonto for the time. Tonto whips off his loincloth to reveal a proud erection. He looks at the shadow cast by his erection and says, "It's 3:15." The Lone Ranger checks his watch. Sure enough, it's 3:15. Later, the Lone Ranger again asks Tonto for the time. Once more he whips off his loincloth, checks his dick's shadow, and replies, "5:20." When the Lone Ranger checks this he finds that, sure enough, it's 5:20. Later that night, the Lone Ranger walks into Tonto's teepee and catches him masturbating furiously. The Lone Ranger asks him what he's doing. Tonto explains, "Me wind'em watch!"

• • • • •

Three cowboys are in a ranch house boasting about their prowess. One says, "I'm so tough, I wrestled a crazy steer to the ground after it'd gored four men!" The second says, "I'm so tough, I once bit the head off a rattlesnake and drank its poison." Then the third cowboy sighs and says, "That fire needs fixing." He goes over to the stove, opens the door and starts stoking it with his dick!

Crime

A group of prisoners are at a rehabilitation meeting. Their first step is to admit their crimes. A prisoner stands up and says, "My name's Danny. I'm in for murder." Another prisoner stands up and says, "My name's Jimmy. I'm in for armed robbery." A third prisoner stands up and says, "Ma' name is Billy-Bob. I'm in here for fucking dogs." All the prisoners make noises of disgust. Danny says, "Jesus, man! And I thought *I* was bad. How low can you go?" Billy-Bob replies, "Well, I did manage to do a dachshund one time…"

• • • • •

A little old lady is being questioned in court. "What happened when the young man sat down next to you on the park bench?" asks the attorney. The little old lady replies, "Well, it was then he started rubbing my thighs." "And did you call the police at this point?" asks the attorney. "No," replies the old lady. "So what happened then?" continues the attorney. "Well, he then started to fondle my bosom," replies the old lady. "And did you call for the police then?"

asks the attorney? "No," replies the little old lady. "What happened after that?" he asks. "Well," says the little old lady. "That's when he started kissing me and suggested we go into the bushes for intercourse." "I see," says the attorney. "And is that when you called for the police?" "No," replies the old lady. "That's when he shouted, 'April Fool!' and I shot the son of a bitch!"

•••••

A woman and a psycho are taking a walk through some deep, dark woods. The woman says, "I'm scared! These woods are really creepy." The psycho replies, "How do you think *I* feel? I've got to walk back all by myself!"

•••••

An escaped convict breaks into a house and ties up a young couple. While the convict ransacks the place, looking for cash, the husband turns to his voluptuous young wife and whispers, "Honey, this guy hasn't seen a woman in years. Cooperate with anything he wants. If he wants to have sex with you, just go along with it and pretend you like it. Our lives depend on it!" "Darling," answers his wife. "I'm so glad you feel that way. While he was tying me up, he told me what a nice firm butt you have!"

•••••

A godfather is on his deathbed and calls his eldest son to him. "Ricardo," he croaks. "I want you to have this family heirloom." Saying this, he pulls out a gun and hands it to his boy. "Gee, Pa," his son replies. "You know I don't like guns. If you want to leave me something, why not give me your watch?" "I see," the indignant godfather replies. "You don't want my gun, huh! So tell me, one day when you get home and find your wife in bed with the mailman, watcha' gonna do? Shoot him, or point at your watch and say, 'Hey, buddy, time's up'!"

Crossings

What do you get if you cross your wife with a pit bull?
Your very last blow job!

What do you get when you cross a yeast infection and an achy-breaky heart? An itchy-twitchy crotch!

What do you get when you cross an elephant with a poodle? A cross-eyed poodle that has to sit on a cushion!

Dating

A boy is going to meet his girlfriend's parents for the first time and has been promised a night of sex afterward. To prepare for the big event he goes to a drugstore and tells the pharmacist that he's going on a hot date with a sex-crazy girl. The pharmacist sells him a ten-pack of condoms and wishes him luck. That night the boy goes over to the girl's parents' house and is shown to the dinner table, where her parents are already seated. The boy offers to say grace and bows his head. A minute passes, and the boy is still deep in prayer. Ten minutes pass and still he is deep in prayer. Finally, after twenty minutes with his head down, his girlfriend leans over and whispers, "I had no idea you were so religious." The boy whispers back, "Yeah—and I had no idea your father was a pharmacist!"

•••••

A couple, John and Mary, have just started dating and are taking a walk in the woods. Mary has to go to the bathroom so she excuses herself and ducks behind a bush. John hears Mary taking off her jeans and panties. He can't resist having a feel, so he pushes his hand through the undergrowth and slides his hand up her thigh. Suddenly his hand touches something long, thick and warm hanging between Mary's legs. "Oh, my God!" shouts John. "Y'mean, you're really a guy?" "No," replies Mary. "It means I'm *really* taking a shit!"

•••••

A girl and her boyfriend are at the back of a movie theater, kissing passionately. They come up for air and the boy says, "I really like kissing you, but would you mind not passing me your chewing gum all the time." "It's not chewing gum," the girl replies. "I've got bronchitis!"

•••••

A mouse and a lion are drinking in a bar when this beautiful female giraffe walks in. "Wow, get a load of her," exclaims the mouse. "I'd sure love some of that!" "Why not try your luck?" the lion suggests. So the mouse goes over to the giraffe and starts chatting her up. They get along really well and, after a short while, they leave together. The next week the lion is in the bar when the mouse staggers in and collapses into a seat. "My God," says the lion. "You look shattered! What the hell happened to you?" "It's that giraffe," replies the mouse. "The giraffe?" says the lion. "But it looked like you two really hit it off." "We did," answers the mouse. "I spent all last week at her house." "So why do you look so exhausted?" asks the lion. The mouse replies, "Because in-between all the kissing and screwing we've been doing, I must've run about a thousand miles!"

•••••

A young Italian girl is about to go on her first date and her grandmother warns her about boys. "They only want one thing," she says. "So don't let him take liberties. Don't let him feel your chest, don't let him touch your legs, don't play with his dick, and don't *ever* let him lie on top of you. If you ever let him lie on you, you will bring disgrace on your family." The girl takes in this information and goes off on her date. When she returns, her grandmother asks her how it went. "Well," says the girl. "I didn't let him feel my body and I didn't play with his dick. But when *I* wouldn't touch it, he got it out and played with it himself." "Mamma mia!" says the grandmother. "Don't tell me you let him get on top of you and bring disgrace to your family?" "Oh, no," the girl replies. "I remembered what you said, so I got on top of him and disgraced *his* family!"

•••••

A young man goes to his girlfriend's house for dinner. On the way there she tells him about an odd family custom— the first person to speak after dinner has to do the dishes. The couple sit down to eat with the girl's parents, and when they've finished everyone sits round the table in silence. The young man doesn't want to do the dishes so he tries to create a comment by kissing his girlfriend full on the mouth. No one utters a word, so the young man puts his hands up his girlfriend's blouse. Still no one says anything. The young man pulls out all the stops: He strips his girl-friend naked and they have sex on the table. Still no one speaks. But the young man is not to be beaten. He tries again but this time he strips his girlfriend's mother and has sex with her. Still no one says a word. The young man sighs. He knows he's beaten and starts to clear the table. He picks up the butter dish and the father jumps out of his chair. "Okay, okay!" he shouts. "I'll do the damn dishes!"

•••••

Bill is on a date with Brandy, the local good-time girl. They're indulging in some heavy petting and Bill has his hand up Brandy's skirt. "Ow!" complains Brandy. "Your ring is hurting me." "I'm not wearing a ring," replies Bill. "That's my watch!"

•••••

Jeff takes a woman out on their first date. The evening is a huge success. At her door Jeff says, "You look so beautiful, you remind me of a beautiful rambling rose. May I call on you tomorrow?" She agrees and the date is made. The next night Jeff knocks on her door. The woman opens it and slaps him across the face. "What was that for?" asks Jeff. "I looked up 'rambling rose' in the encyclopedia last night," the woman replies. "It said it was not suited to bedding, but was excellent for rooting up against a garden wall!"

•••••

Three men had been on blind dates the previous evening and they all tried to guess the professions of their partners.

The first thought his date had been a nurse because she'd said, "Lie back and relax—this won't hurt a bit." The second decided his date must have been a schoolteacher. She'd said, "Do it again and again until you get it right." The third figured his date must have been a stewardess. All she'd said was, "Put this over your mouth and nose, and continue to breathe normally!"

Death and the Afterlife

How can you tell if your husband is dead? The sex is the same, but you get the remote.

•••••

How can you tell if your wife is dead? The sex is the same, but the dishes pile up.

•••••

George Bush dies and goes to hell. The Devil tells him, "I'm short on space and I've got three people here who weren't quite as bad as you. I'll let one of them go, and you can take their place. As a favor I'll even let you decide who leaves." First, the Devil takes George to a room where Richard Nixon is bobbing in a pool of water. "No," says George. "I wouldn't like that—I'm not a good swimmer." Next, the Devil leads George to a room where Tony Blair is hammering a never-ending pile of rocks. "No," says George. "I wouldn't like that much." The Devil opens the final door. Inside, Bill Clinton is tied to a bench with Monica Lewinsky bent over him giving him a blow job.

George says, "That looks good—I'll take it." "Finally!" exclaims the Devil. "Okay, Monica, you're free to go!"

• • • • •

Joe and Hank die and go to heaven. Saint Peter tells them that they will each get a car, depending on how faithful they were in life. Hank's record is very good: He was married for 24 years and was completely faithful, so he gets a Rolls-Royce. Joe, on the other hand, had five affairs during his marriage and only gets a third-hand VW Beetle. A week later Joe is driving through heaven when he passes Hank, who is crying by the roadside. "What's the matter?" asks Joe, "I thought you'd be really enjoying that Rolls-Royce." "I was," sobs Hank. "But then I saw my wife on a skateboard!"

• • • • •

A husband and wife are having a bitter argument. The husband yells, "When you die, I'm getting you a headstone that reads, 'Here Lies My Wife—Cold As Ever.'" "Yeah?" she replies. "Well, when you die, yours will read, 'Here Lies My Husband—Stiff At Last'!"

• • • • •

Two teenage boys, Luke and Paul, die in an accident and go to heaven. When they arrive, they notice that everyone has a clock on their forehead. A passing angel explains. "These clocks show how many times you masturbated in your lifetime," says the angel. "The faster the clock, the greater the impurity." Luke looks at Paul's forehead and sure enough, the hands of his clock are turning quite quickly. Paul looks at Luke's clock, but can't see one. He turns to the angel and says, "Hey, where's my buddy's clock?" The angel answers, "Oh, we borrowed it. Our office air-conditioning is broken—we're using his clock as a fan!"

Disabilities

A young man goes to a bar, where he meets a girl in a wheelchair who has lost both her legs in an accident. The couple really like each other and the girl invites him back to her place. The only trouble is, her dad's at home so they have to go in the garden. "I'll tell you what to do," says the girl. "Pick me up out of the wheelchair and carry me over to that tree." The man follows her instructions and she gets a good grip on a branch and uses her upper body muscles to lower herself up and down on him. The man can't believe it. He has a fantastic time. Afterward he carries her back to her wheelchair and takes her to the door. At that moment the girl's father appears, takes him inside and says, "I saw what you were doing with my daughter just then." The young man thinks he's in for it, but the father suddenly shakes him by the hand. "What are you doing?" asks the young man. "I thought you saw what I was doing?" "I did," says the girl's father. "Every other bastard she's brought home left her hanging in the tree!"

•••••

A deaf-mute man goes into a drugstore to buy a pack of condoms. He tries explaining what he wants to the sales-clerk in sign language, but the clerk can't understand. Eventually the deaf-mute resorts to a demonstration. He unzips his fly, pulls his penis out, flops it on the counter and lays a five-dollar bill next to it. "Ah!" says the clerk, who then unzips his own fly, flops his penis on the counter and pockets the deaf-mute's money. The deaf-mute is furious and starts banging the counter. "Hey!" says the clerk. "If you can't afford to lose—don't gamble!"

• • • • •

A man is driving through the countryside when he stops to buy some coffee from a roadside eatery. While he's drinking he notices an old couple facing each other outside a farmhouse. The old lady is playing with her breasts while the old man is masturbating furiously. "What the hell!" the man exclaims. He turns to the woman serving coffee and asks, "Have you seen what that old couple are doing?" "Ignore them," she replies. "It's just the Robertson's arguing again—they're both deaf. She's telling him to milk the cows and he's telling her to fuck off!"

• • • • •

A woman is walking along the beach when she sees a man with no arms or legs lying in the sand, crying. She asks him what's wrong and he says he's upset because he's never been kissed before. She kisses him and continues on walking. An hour later she walks back up the beach and finds the man crying again. The man says he's upset because no one's ever given him oral sex. Feeling sorry for him, the woman obliges and then goes up the beach again. Later on she strolls back the same way and finds the man, still crying his eyes out. "So, what's wrong this time?" she asks him. "I'm crying because I've never been screwed before," replies the armless, legless man. "Well, you are now," replies the woman. "The tide's coming in!"

•••••

After a whirlwind romance John gets married. However, he has a big secret he's been keeping from his fiancée—his right leg has been amputated below the knee. John is very nervous about revealing this secret, but on the day of the wedding he tells his bride that he's got a big surprise for her. That evening in the honeymoon suite he gets into bed and slips off his false limb. His bride then comes in, strips off and climbs into bed. "Now," she says. "What was that big surprise you said I had coming?" John gulps and guides her hand under the bed-covers to rest on the end of his stump. "My!" she exclaims. "That's a big one! Don't worry, hand over the Vaseline and I'll see what I can do."

Doctor's Office

A beautiful woman walks into a doctor's office. The doctor, being an over-sexed pervert, decides to make the most of it. He tells her to take off her dress and starts rubbing her thighs. "Do you know what I'm doing?" he asks. "Checking for abnormalities?" replies the woman. The doctor then tells her to take off her bra and starts rubbing her breasts. "Do you know what I'm doing now?" he asks. The woman replies, "Checking for lumps, I suppose." Finally, the doctor tells her to take off her underwear, lays her on the table and starts having sex with her. "Do you know what I'm doing now?" asks the doctor. "Yes," replies the woman, "Getting crabs—that's why I'm here!"

•••••

A doctor and his wife have a big fight over breakfast. They are arguing about their sex life: Each thinks the other is a lousy bed partner. The fight escalates and the doctor storms off to his office. A few hours later he's calmed down, so he calls home to apologize but the phone rings and rings. He's about to hang up when his wife answers. "What took you so long to answer?" asks the doctor. His wife says, "I was in bed." "A little late to be in bed, isn't it?" says the doctor. His wife replies, "I was getting a second opinion!"

•••••

A doctor is having sex with a married woman when her husband bursts in on them, brandishing a shotgun. The doctor panics and shouts, "It's not what it looks like—I was only taking her temperature." "Oh, yes?" replies the husband, aiming his gun. "Then you'd better hope it's got numbers on it when you take it out!"

•••••

A girl goes to see her doctor for an annual checkup. She takes off her shirt and the doctor notices a big rash in an "H" shape on the girl's chest. The girl explains where it came from. "My boyfriend likes to keep his T-shirt on when we make love," she says. "And he goes to Harvard, hence the 'H' mark." "Well, it's nothing serious," says the doctor and sends her on her way. The next year the girl returns and this time the doctor finds an "S"-shaped rash on the girl's chest. "My boyfriend likes to make love with his T-shirt on," she explains, "and he goes to Stanford." Again the doctor tells her not to worry and sends her on her way. The next year the same thing happens, except that this time the rash is "M"-shaped "So," says the doctor. "I assume your current boyfriend goes to Michigan?" "No," she replies, "My new *girlfriend* goes to Washington!"

• • • • •

A man is having his eyes tested. "You must stop masturbating so frequently," remarks the optician. "Why?" asks the man. "Is it ruining my eyesight?" "No," the optician replies. "But it's upsetting the other patients in the waiting room!"

• • • • •

A woman goes to her doctor for a checkup. The doctor asks her to strip, do a handstand and open her legs. The woman is mystified by this, but follows the doctor's instructions. She is further confused when the doctor props his chin between her legs and stares in the mirror. "What exactly are you doing?" asks the woman. "Nothing much," he replies. "I just wondered what I'd look like with a goatee…"

• • • • •

A young woman goes to her doctor with a scalded belly. While he's examining her, he also finds large lumps of wax in her navel. "Can you explain how all this wax got here?" he asks. "How can I put it?" the young woman replies. "Y'see, my boyfriend likes to eat by candlelight…"

• • • • •

Mrs. Smith goes to the doctor for an exam. After her examination the doctor says, "Overall you're very healthy for a woman your age. However, you're overweight and bordering on the clinically obese." "*Obese*?" replies the offended Mrs. Smith. "I demand a second opinion!" "Okay," says the doctor. "You're fucking ugly, too!"

Domestic Appliances

Did you hear about the new home appliance? You screw it on the bed and it does all the housework!

Dreams

Due to bad weather a number of flights are canceled and the airport hotel starts to fill up. In fact, it's so overcrowded that three men find themselves sleeping in the same bed. When they wake up the next morning the man on the right side of the bed says, "I had a very vivid dream last night. It was absolutely fantastic. I dreamt a beautiful woman was jacking me off all night long." "Hey," says the man on the left side of the bed, "I had exactly the same dream." "You're both disgusting," says the man in the middle. "I had a lovely dream—all about skiing!"

•••••

One morning a woman tells her husband about an odd dream she had. "I was at a penis auction," she says. "And big penises were going for $1,000 and little ones were $100." "Really?" her husband replies. "And what about a penis like mine?" "No bids," his wife answers. Hurt by this comment the husband decides to get his revenge. The next morning he says to his wife, "I had a dream about a vagina auction last night. Really big loose vaginas were going for $1 and small tight ones were $10,000." "Oh, yes?" replies his wife. "And what about a vagina like mine?" "That wasn't for sale," the husband answers. "They were holding the auction in it!"

Drink

A drunk is out looking for a brothel but he takes a wrong turn and ends up in a podiatrist's. The receptionist shows him to a couch in a curtained cubicle and tells him to get ready. The drunk strips off and playfully sticks his erection through the gap in the curtains. He hears someone scream, "Oh, my God! That's not a foot!" "God damn!" says the drunk. "I didn't know they had a minimum…"

•••••

A drunk staggers into the back of a cab. He leans toward the driver and asks, "Here, have you got room for a lobster and a bottle of wine on your front seat?" "I think so," says the driver. "Good," the drunk replies, and throws up.

•••••

A group of young men are in the bar when a drunk shuffles in and starts shouting. He points to one of the guys and says, "Hey, I screwed your mom!" The guy ignores him. "Yeah!" shouts the drunk. "I've had her up the ass as well!" Again the guy does his best to ignore him. The drunk gets his dick out and waves it around. "See this?" he shouts. "That's been in your mom's mouth!" The guy can't contain himself any longer. "Oh, go home, Dad!" he shouts. "You're drunk!"

• • • • •

A man walks into a bar with his girlfriend. A drunk looks at the girl and says, "If you were my woman, I'd lick you from top to bottom like a lollipop." The man is furious and gets ready to punch the drunk, but his girlfriend stops him, telling him she doesn't want a scene. The drunk then walks over and tries to give her a big sloppy kiss. The man pulls him off and is about to hit him, when the girlfriend pulls him away. "If that guy even looks at you again, I'm going to kill him!" shouts the man. After a couple of minutes, the drunk comes over and says, "If you were my woman, I'd turn you upside-down, fill your pussy with beer and drink you dry with one swallow." The man takes the girl's arm and walks her out of the bar. "I thought you were going to beat him up," says the girl. "I was," the man replies. "But if he can drink that much beer, he's a better man than I am!"

• • • • •

Betty has too much to drink at a party. She goes for a stroll and ends up passing out in a pasture. She opens her eyes and sees a cow standing over her. "Okay, boys," she slurs. "But one at a time…"

• • • • •

Three men are discussing a night out. "I was so drunk last night," says one, "I crawled home and pissed in my bed."

"That's nothing," says the second, "I was so drunk last night, I went home and woke up naked in my front garden." "I can beat that," says the third man, "I was so drunk last night I went home and spent the whole night blowing chunks." "Well, there's nothing unusual in that," says the second man. "I threw up as well." "No," the third man replies. "'Chunks' is the name of my dog!"

• • • • •

Two drunks, Jeff and Mike, are in a bar. Mike gets up to go to the restroom. Suddenly there's a sound of screaming from the restroom. Jeff rushes in to see what's wrong and finds Mike sobbing on the floor. "It was terrible," he says. "I sat down and took a crap, but every time I tried to flush the toilet something reached up and squeezed my balls." Jeff looks in the toilet stall and says, "You moron… You were sitting on the mop bucket!"

Elephants

What's the world's biggest drawback? An elephant's foreskin!

• • • • •

Two old ladies go to the zoo and see a male elephant with a huge erection rampaging around the enclosure. One of the old ladies says, "Gracious, do you think he'll charge?" The other old lady looks at the erection and says, "Well, yes. I think he'd be entitled to!"

•••••

What did the elephant say to the nude man? "It's cute, but can it pick up peanuts?"

•••••

What does an elephant use for a tampon? A sheep!

•••••

A man shuffles into a doctor's office and asks to be examined. It turns out he has severe bruising of the buttocks and a ruptured anus. "How did this happen?" asks the doctor. "It's very embarrassing," says the man. "But when I was on safari I was raped by a bull elephant." "How extraordinary," the doctor remarks. "But from the little I know about the subject I understood that male elephants have a long, very thin, penis." "They do," sniffs the man. "But this one fingered me first."

Excuses, Excuses

A husband emerges from the bathroom naked and climbs into bed. As usual his wife says, "No sex tonight, dear. I have a headache." "Perfect," says the husband. "I was just in the bathroom powdering my penis with aspirin. How do you want it? Orally, or as a suppository?"

•••••

A guy wakes up in the middle of the night, rolls over and drops an aspirin down his wife's throat. She wakes up and yells, "What the hell are you doing?" "I'm just giving you an aspirin for your headache," he replies. "I haven't *got* a headache!" she shouts. "Great," he says. "Then let's fuck!"

•••••

A husband and wife are in bed. The husband asks his wife if she wants sex. "I'm sorry, honey," she says. "But I've got a gynecologist's appointment tomorrow and I want to stay fresh." After a few moments the husband says, "So do you have a dental appointment too?"

•••••

A husband wakes his wife up at two in the morning. "I'm feeling really horny," he says. "Any chance of a blow job?" "Aw, I'm too tired," his wife groans. "Tell you what, why don't you jerk off into that glass and I'll drink it in the morning?"

Extreme Weather

What did the hurricane say to the coconut tree? "Hang onto your nuts, this is going to be one hell of a blow job!"

•••••

A man is driving down a road in Alaska when his car breaks down. He calls a mechanic, who arrives shortly after. The mechanic opens the hood, peers at the engine, and says, "Looks like you've blown a seal." The man replies, "Nah, it's just frost on my moustache!"

•••••

The President wakes up one morning and looks out of the White House window to see "The President Sucks" written in the snow in urine. Furious, he calls in the FBI and demands the perpetrators be found. Later, an FBI agent returns and says, "Well, sir, we've got bad news, and worse news. The bad news is, we had the urine analyzed and it belongs to the Vice President." "Jesus!" the President exclaims. "So, what's the worse news?" The agent replies, "The message appears to be in your wife's handwriting!"

· · · · ·

A young couple hire a Swiss chalet for a romantic winter vacation. On their first day the man goes to chop some wood. When he gets back, he says, "Darling, my hands are freezing." His wife replies, "Well, put them between my thighs. They'll warm up soon." The next day the man goes out for more wood. When he returns, he says, "Darling, my hands are freezing." Again, his wife replies, "Well, put them between my thighs. They'll warm up soon." The next day the man goes out for yet more wood. He comes back and says, "Darling, my hands are freezing." His wife replies, "Again! Don't your fucking ears ever get cold!"

· · · · ·

A young polar bear asks his mother, "Am I a real polar bear?" "Of course you are," his mother replies. The young polar bear then asks his father the same question, "Dad, am I a real polar bear?" "Yes," says his dad. "You are a real polar bear." The young polar bear then asks his parents, "Are Grandma and Grandpa real polar bears?" "Yes," his parents reply. "So are all my relatives real polar bears?" the young polar bear asks. "Yes, they're all real polar bears," answers his dad. "Why do you ask?" "Because," replies the young polar bear, "I am fucking *freezing*!"

• • • • •

Why are hurricanes usually named after women? When they come, they're wild and wet. When they go, they take your house and car!

Farmers

A farmer comes home from the fields early and sees a light on in his bedroom. Suspecting his wife is up to no good, he creeps into the bedroom with a shotgun and finds his farmhand naked, in bed with his wife. The farmhand stands up and shouts, "Don't shoot! For God's sake, give me a chance!" The farmer aims his gun and replies, "Okay, I'll give you a chance… now swing 'em!"

• • • • •

A farmer insists on meeting his daughters' boyfriends before they're allowed out on dates. One evening the doorbell rings and a boy calls for one of the girls. "Hi, my name's Joe," says the boy. "I'm here for Flo. We're going to the show. Is she ready to go?" The father calls down Flo and off they go. Another boy arrives, "My name's Eddie, I'm here for Betty. We're gonna get some spaghetti. Is she ready?" The father calls down Betty and off they go. A third young man arrives and says, "Hi, my name's Tucker…" and the farmer shoots him.

• • • • •

A farmer is lying in bed with his wife. He starts rubbing her breasts and says, "If only we could milk these, we could get rid of the cow." Then he rubs her backside and says, "And if this laid eggs, we could get rid of the chickens." His wife leans over and rubs his penis, "…And if we saw a bit more action from this, we could get rid of your brother!"

•••••

A farmer takes his son to market to buy a cow. The farmer pokes the cow all over, strokes its sides, looks in every nook and cranny, and even lifts its tail so he can peer up its ass. "Y'see, boy," he explains. "You have to give it a real good going over before you know if it's worth paying money for." The next day the boy runs up to his father and says, "Pa! Pa! I just saw ma and the mailman behind the barn—I think he's planning on buying her!"

•••••

A farmer catches his young son coming out of the woods with the neighbor's daughter. He asks the boy what they've been up to, and the son confesses they've been having wild sex. The father tells him not to do it again, but gives the boy a cookie as a reward for telling the truth. The next day he catches his son doing exactly the same thing. Again, he questions him, gets an answer and again, gives the boy a cookie for telling the truth. The following day the same thing happens and again, the son is told off, but given a reward for speaking the truth. The day after the son and the neighbor's daughter are caught yet again. This time the father goes into the kitchen and starts frying eggs. "Eggs?" asks the mother. "What happened to the cookies?" The father replies, "He can't keep that up, living on cookies!"

•••••

A man falls in love with a farmer's daughter. Unfortunately the farmer doesn't think much of the man so he gives him some "impossible" tasks to perform. "Before you can marry my daughter," he says, "you must first jump the barbed-wire fence, then swim the river, then go and have sex with the cow in the barn." The man is surprised at these requests, but manages to complete the tasks with ease. The farmer is astonished. "Actually, there are some more tests you have to do as well," he says. "To marry my daughter, you must harvest a field of potatoes in one night, fix my rusty old tractor, and then go have sex with the cow in the barn." This time the young man has more trouble, but eventually the tasks are completed. The farmer still can't believe it, so he sets more tasks. Now the young man must divert the river, put up one hundred miles of fencing, build a new farmhouse and then go and have sex with the cow in the barn. The man struggles to complete the tasks, but eventually he prevails. "Hell!" exclaims the farmer. "If you can do all that, I'd be glad to have you as a son-in-law. Of course you can marry my daughter!" The man replies, "Screw your daughter—how much for the cow?"

•••••

A man goes to his doctor with a broken leg. "How did this happen?" asks the doctor. "Twenty years ago I went on vacation to a farm," replies the man. "The farmer had a beautiful young daughter and on the first night I was there she came to my room in her nightgown and asked if there was anything I'd like to give her. I told her I couldn't think of anything. On the second night she returned and asked if I was sure there wasn't anything I could give her. Again, I said I still couldn't think of anything. Then, on the third night, she came back and asked if I was positive there wasn't anything I could give her. Again, I said, no—I still couldn't think of anything." "So what's that got to do with breaking your leg?" the doctor asks. "Well," replies the man. "This morning I was up a ladder when I suddenly realized what I *could* have given her!"

• • • • •

A salesman knocks on the door of a farmhouse, which is answered by a little boy. "Is your mother in?" asks the salesman. "Yes," the boy replies. "She's out back, screwing the goat." The salesman is appalled to hear this news. He goes around to the backyard and sure enough, there's a lady on her hands and knees being screwed by a goat. "Holy crap!" exclaims the salesman. He turns to the boy and asks, "Doesn't that bother you, kid?" The boy replies, "Naaa-haaa-haaa…."

• • • • •

John goes to see his farmer friend. One morning John gets up early and decides to fix breakfast. Later the farmer comes downstairs and finds John covered in white liquid, carrying a bucket. "Surprise!" says John. "I got up early and milked the cow for you." "Surprise!" replies the farmer. "We don't have a cow—it's a bull!"

Farmers: Over-Familiarity with Sheep

A farmer's wife gives him a plate of grass for his dinner. "What the hell's this?" he asks. The wife replies, "If it's good enough for your girlfriend, it's good enough for you!"

•••••

A farmer and his wife found themselves in a love triangle, but the solution was surprisingly simple—they ate the sheep.

•••••

How does a farmer make a U-turn? He winks at it.

•••••

How does a farmer find a sheep in the long grass? Satisfying.

•••••

They just discovered a new use for sheep in Wales—wool.

•••••

What do you call a farmer with forty lovers? A shepherd.

•••••

What do you call a farmer with a sheep under each arm? A pimp.

•••••

What do you call a farmer with a sheep under one arm and a goat under the other? Bi-sexual.

•••••

What goes, "…205, 206, 207, hello, darling… 209, 210…?" A farmer counting his sheep!

•••••

What was the farmer's defense in court? "Honest, Your Honor, I was just helping the sheep over the fence…"

•••••

Why do farmers have sex with their sheep on the edge of mountains? So they'll push back harder!

Farting

A male fly and a female fly are feeding on a cowpatty when the male fly farts. The female fly says, "Do you mind—I'm eating!"

•••••

A man is walking down a beach one evening when a prostitute approaches him. "Thirty bucks for a quickie?" she asks. The man agrees and they go under a pier, where they have sex on the sand. The next evening the man goes back to find the prostitute and, again, they go under the pier for sex. Everything proceeds as the night before except this time the prostitute lets off a huge fart halfway through their session. When it's over, the man hands her thirty-five dollars. "What's that for?" the woman asks. "The thirty is for the sex," replies the man. "And the extra five is for blowing the sand off my balls!"

• • • • •

A young man goes to pick up his date. She's not ready, so he has to sit in the living room with her mother. The man has a bad case of wind and needs to relieve some pressure. The family dog jumps up on the couch next to him and the man decides that he can let out a little fart and, if anyone notices, they'll think the dog did it. He farts, and the mother yells, "Spot, get down from there!" The man thinks, "Great, they think the dog did it." He releases another fart, and again the mother yells for the dog to get down. This goes on for a couple more farts. Finally, the mother yells, "Dammit, Spot! Get down before that bastard craps on you!"

• • • • •

An old couple have lived happily together for many years. The only friction in their marriage is caused by the husband's habit of farting every morning. The wife complains and often warns her husband that one day he'll "Fart his guts out." However, he ignores her and keeps on farting. One day after cleaning out a chicken the wife decides to play a trick on her windy husband. That night she takes the giblets and, when her husband has fallen asleep, slips them under the bedsheets, between his legs. The next morning she wakes up and asks her husband how he slept. "Fine, till this morning," he replies. "Then I discovered you were right all along; I *did* fart my guts out." "Are you going to see the doctor?" asks his wife. "Nah," her husband replies. "It took a while, but I managed to poke them all back up again!"

•••••

Bill goes to his doctor suffering from chronic flatulence. The doctor asks him to take off his pants and lie down on the couch. Then, to Bill's horror, he produces a six-foot pole. "What are you going to do with that?" asks Bill. "I'm going to open a window," the doctor replies.

•••••

Fart in church, and you'll sit in your own pew.

•••••

Two old ladies are discussing the benefits of stockings over tights. "I much prefer stockings," says one. "Do you find them more elegant?" asks the other. "Oh, yes," replies the first. "And if I fart wearing tights, I usually blow my slippers off!"

Fat

Did you hear about the 150-pound man who had 75-pound testicles? He was half nuts!

•••••

I knew a woman who was so fat she had to use a mattress as a tampon.

•••••

Why's a fat woman like a scooter? They're both fun to ride but you wouldn't want your friends to see you on one!

Feminine Hygiene

Why do women pierce their belly buttons? It's a good place to hang an air freshener!

•••••

One morning in Eden, God is looking for Adam and Eve, but can't find them. Later in the day He sees Adam and asks where he and Eve have been hiding. Adam tells him, "This morning Eve and I were in the bamboo grove making love for the first time." God replies, "Adam, you have sinned. I knew this would happen. Where is Eve now?" Adam says, "She's down by the river, washing herself out." "Oh, that's great," groans God. "Now all the fish will smell funny..."

•••••

A man gets married, but decides to spend his wedding night doing some fishing in a lake by the honeymoon hotel. The best man comes across the groom as he casts his line. "What are you doing out here?" he asks. "Shouldn't you be with your wife, giving her a good time?" "I can't," replies the groom. "She's got gonorrhea." "Well, what about anal sex?" suggests the best man. "Can't do that either," moans the groom. "She's got diarrhea, too." "Yeeuch!" exclaims the best man, "Well, there's always oral sex..." "Nope," the groom replies. "She's also got pyorrhea." "Well, for God's sake!" says the best man. "What the hell did you marry her for?" The groom casts his line again and replies, "The worms!"

•••••

A man is sitting on his sofa throwing peanuts into his mouth when one of them gets lodged up his nose. Neither the man nor his wife can do anything to shift it and they start to get desperate. Luckily the couple's daughter and her boyfriend return home from a trip to the movies. The boyfriend is studying to be a doctor and he manages to stick his fingers up the man's nose and massage the peanut out. Later, the wife remarks, "It was lucky he's having medical training. I wonder what he's going to become, a GP or a surgeon?" "I don't know," her husband replies. "But by the smell of his fingers, there's a good chance he's going to become our son-in-law!"

• • • • •

A woman gets on a bus and sits down opposite an incredibly attractive man. She tries to flirt with him, but he doesn't seem interested. She pouts at him, but gets no response and so she unbuttons her blouse to reveal some cleavage—still no reaction. Finally, she pulls out all the stops—she pulls up her skirt and opens her legs to reveal she's not wearing any underwear. The man sniffs the air, then stands up and pulls out a collapsible white stick. "That was quick," he comments. "It's usually half an hour to the fish market!"

• • • • •

A young woman is on a train when an old man sits opposite her. The old man gets a bag of prawns out of his pocket and starts eating them, throwing the shells on the floor around the young woman's feet, and occasionally in her lap. When he's done, he twists up the bag and throws it at the young woman's head. She picks up the bag, collects all the pieces of shell in it, and throws the whole thing out the window. The young woman then pulls on the emergency stop cord. "You silly bitch," says the old man. "You'll get a $50 fine!" To which the woman replies, "Yes, but when the police smell your fingers, you'll get five years!"

•••••

What's the logo for the new Irish tampon? "We may not be number 1, but we're still up there!"

•••••

Ted and Joan are on vacation in Australia. Every day they go for a walk on the beach and every day they see a huge fat woman, completely naked, sitting on the sand with her legs wide open, eating a slice of watermelon. This goes on for a week until one day Joan goes over to say hello. "It must be very liberating and refreshing to let the fresh air get to your private areas," she remarks. "Wouldn't know about that," replies the fat woman. "I'm just trying to keep the damn flies off my watermelon!"

•••••

Three prisoners are locked in a cell. One takes out a harmonica and says, "At least I can play a little music to pass the time." The second prisoner pulls out a pack of cards and says, "We can play games, too." The third man produces a packet of tampons. "Those aren't much use," remarks the first prisoner. "Yes, they are," replies the third prisoner. "On the packet it says we can use them to swim, play tennis and ski!"

•••••

Why do tampons have strings hanging off the end of them? So you can floss after eating!

Fishing

One morning a man turns to his wife and says, "It's a great day for a fishing trip. You, me and the dog will spend the day by the river." "I don't want to go fishing," complains the wife. "It's so boring." "Listen," replies her husband. "You've got a choice: you can either come fishing with me and the dog, or you can give me a blow job, or take it up the ass. Now you think about it while I get my fishing kit." The wife thinks about it. She decides she really doesn't want to go fishing or take it up the ass, so when her husband comes back, she opts to give him a blow job. The husband unzips his fly and his wife puts his dick in her mouth. "Yeeuch!" she shouts, spitting it out again. "Your dick tastes like shit!" "Yeah," replies her husband. "The dog didn't want to go fishing either!"

Food and Eating Out

Fred goes to a cafe and orders hot chili, but the waitress tells him that the man at the next table got the last bowl. He gets a cup of coffee instead, then notices that the man on the next table has finished eating, but left his chili bowl full. Fred goes over. "If you're not going to eat that, can I have it?" he asks. "Sure," the man replies. So Fred takes the bowl back to his table and starts spooning it down. He gets halfway through when he sees a dead mouse in the chili and pukes his meal back up. The other man calls out, "That's about as far as I got, too!"

• • • • •

George is in a restaurant when he knocks his spoon off the table. Immediately a waiter comes along and takes a fresh spoon out of his pocket. "That's very efficient," says George. "Thank you, sir," replies the waiter. "All the staff carry a spare spoon in case of emergencies." George then notices a string hanging out of the waiter's fly. "Do you know you have a piece of string hanging out of your pants?" he asks. "Why yes, sir," replies the waiter. "It's attached to my penis. If I have to answer a call of nature, I can go to the bathroom and pull my penis out with the string. We find this much faster and more hygienic than the normal method." "I'm extremely impressed," says George. "But tell me, how do you get your penis back inside your pants without touching it?" The waiter replies, "Well, sir, I usually poke mine back with a spoon!"

• • • • •

A man goes into an ice cream parlor. Outside is a notice which promises that the parlor can create any flavor on the spot. The man goes up to the counter and says, "I want ice cream that tastes like fish and chips." The parlor owner steps into a back room and five minutes later reappears with a cone of ice cream. The man takes a lick, but complains he can only taste fish. "Turn it around," says the owner. The man does so, takes another lick and discovers the other side tastes like chips. "Okay," says the man. "How about ice cream that tastes like liver and onions?" The parlor owner goes into his back room and, minutes later, he returns with another cone. The man takes a lick and can taste only onions. "What about the liver?" he asks. "Turn it around," says the owner. Sure enough the man has a lick from the other side of the cone and he can taste liver. "Okay," says the man. "Now for a real test. Make me an ice cream that tastes like my wife's pussy." The parlor owner goes into his back room and comes back with a pussy-flavored cone. The man takes a lick and says, "Urrgh! This tastes like crap!" The owner replies, "Turn it around."

•••••

A man walks into a delicatessen and asks for a tub of vanilla ice cream, a tub of strawberry and a tub of chocolate. "Sorry," says the woman at the counter. "We're out of chocolate ice cream." "In that case," says the man, "I'll have a tub of tutti-frutti, a tub of coffee and a tub of chocolate." "I just told you we don't have any chocolate ice cream," says the woman. "Okay," the man replies. "Then I'll have a tub of rocky road, a tub of mango and a tub of chocolate." The woman is getting annoyed now. "Listen," she says. "What does the V-A-N in vanilla spell?" "Van," the man replies. "And what does the S-T-R-A-W in strawberry spell?" asks the woman. "Straw," answers the man. "Okay, so what does the F-U-C-K in chocolate spell?" she asks. "There's no 'fuck' in chocolate!" replies the man. "That's what I've been trying to tell you!" shouts the woman.

•••••

A mother cooks some deer for dinner. When she and her family sit down to eat, her little boy asks if they're eating beef. "No," replies his father. The little girl asks if they're eating pork. "No," her father replies. "So what *are* we eating?" asks the little boy. "I'll give you a clue," says his father. "It's what your mother sometimes calls me." The children spit out their food. "Christ!" shouts the little boy, "They're feeding us assholes!"

·····

A small boy is sitting on a park bench eating chocolate bars. Sitting opposite, an old man watches as the boy scarfs down six bars and makes a start on the seventh. "That's a lot of chocolate," remarks the old man. "So much isn't good for you—it'll rot your teeth, make you fat and give you heart trouble." "Oh, yeah?" replies the small boy. "Well, my grandpa lived to be a 110." "Really?" says the old man. "And did he eat seven chocolate bars at a time?" "No," replies the boy. "Mostly he just minded his own fucking business!"

·····

A woman goes to a diner in a small Missouri town. She orders fried chicken but eats too fast and starts to choke on a bone. Billy-Bob and Leroy are sitting at the next table. They see what's happening and leap into action. Leroy undoes his coveralls, drops his jockey shorts and bends over. Billy-Bob then crouches behind him and starts licking his asshole. The woman sees this and pukes, dislodging the bone at the same time. "Howwee!" cries Billy-Bob. "I tells you, that "hind-lick" maneuver will do it every time!"

Fortuneteller

Billy goes to the local fair and tries out the fortuneteller. The old woman offers to read his palm. "Your hand tells me many things about you," she says. "You are not married." "No, I'm not," Billy replies. "And you have not had a girlfriend for many, many months," she continues. "That's right," says Billy. "In fact, you spend many lonely evenings by yourself," says the old woman. "That's incredible," says Billy. "Y'mean you can tell all that just from reading my love line?" "No," the old woman replies. "But the blisters and friction burns on your fingers are a dead giveaway!"

Gambling

A boy and his grandpa are watching horseraces on television. The boy asks if he can place a bet. The grandpa says, "Well, that depends. Can you touch your asshole with the end of your dick?" "No," replies the boy. "Then you're not old enough to gamble," replies the grandpa. "Now go and get me a copy of the *Daily Racing Form*." The boy hurries to the newsstand to buy the paper and while he's there he also buys a scratch-card that wins him $50,000. Excitedly he runs home and tells his grandpa the good news. "Y'know what?" says the grandpa. "Seeing as you bought that card with my money we ought to split the prize." "Grandpa," replies the boy. "Can you touch your asshole with the end of your dick?" "Why of course I can," replies the grandpa. "Good!" says the boy. "Then go fuck yourself!"

• • • • •

A man loses all his cash at a Las Vegas casino and tries to beg a ride to the airport from a cab driver. He promises to send back the cab fare when he gets home, but the cab driver very rudely tells him to go to hell. A year later the man returns and sees the same cab driver waiting last in line at a taxi stand. To get his revenge the man approaches the first driver at the taxi stand and asks, "How much to the airport?" "Fifteen dollars," is the reply. "And how much for a blow job on the way?" asks the man. The cab driver is disgusted, "Get away from my car, you pervert!" he shouts. The man continues down the line of cars, asking each driver the price to the airport and how much he charges for a blow job. Each driver is disgusted and tells him to get lost. Finally, the man approaches the last cab in line and speaks to the driver who'd been rude to him. "How much to the airport?" asks the man. "Fifteen dollars," replies the driver. The man gets into the car and off they go. As they pass the line of waiting drivers, the man leans out of the window with a grin on his face and gives them the thumbs-up.

Gay Time

A gay man goes to a doctor's office convinced that he's pregnant. "How could you possibly be pregnant?" asks the doctor. "Who's the father?" "What do you think I have?" asks the gay man. "Eyes in the back of my head?"

• • • • •

A gay man walks into a delicatessen and asks for a large stick of salami. "Would you like it sliced, sir?" asks the shopkeeper. The man exclaims, "What do you think I am, a slot machine?"

•••••

A thug goes into a bar looking for a fight. He stands on a chair and shouts, "Anyone on the left side of the bar is an asshole! Anyone want to disagree?" No one moves a muscle, so the thug shouts, "Anyone on the right side of the bar is a fag! Anyone want to disagree?" No one on the right side of the bar moves, but a little old man on the left side stands up. "Hey!" shouts the thug. "You looking for trouble?" "No," replies the old man. "It's just that I appear to be sitting on the wrong side of the room!"

•••••

After years of avoiding the subject, Ricardo decides it's time to come out to his Italian mother. He finds her in the kitchen and tells her he's a homosexual. "You mean, you're gay?" asks his mother tearfully. "Yes, Mamma," he replies. "You mean you do all those dirty sex things with other men?" "I do, Mamma," says Ricardo. "You mean, you even put other men's genitals in your mouth?" asks his mother. "Yes, Mamma," he says. "I see," she says. She wipes away a tear then starts hitting Ricardo with a ladle. "So you put men's dicks in your goddamn mouth and you have the nerve to complain about the taste of my lasagna?"

•••••

Bruce goes out to work while his boyfriend, Cyril, stays at home every day doing the housework. One day Bruce comes home and finds Cyril with his ass in the fridge. "What are you doing, Cyril darling?" he asks. "Hi, Brucie," replies Cyril, "I was just fixing you something nice and cool to slip into!"

• • • • •

Did you hear about the gay cowboy? He rode into town and shot up the sheriff!

Did you hear about the gay truckers? They exchanged loads!

Did you hear about the two gay guys who had an argument in a bar? They went outside to exchange blows!

Did you hear about the two queer judges? They tried each other!

Have you heard about the new breakfast cereal called "Queerios"? You pour on the milk and they eat themselves!

How do you spot a gay bank robber? He's the one that ties up the safe and blows the security guard!

How can you tell if you're entering a gay household? The welcome mat reads, "Please Wipe Your Knees."

How do you get four gay men on a barstool? Turn it upside down.

How do you make a fruit cordial? Compliment his shoes.

How many gay men does it take to put in a light bulb? Only one—but it takes an entire emergency room to remove it!

How many gay men does it take to change a lightbulb? Seven. One to change the bulb and six to shriek, "Faaaaaaabulous!"

• • • • •

Little Lucy is playing in the garden when she spots two spiders having sex. "Daddy, what are those two spiders doing?" she asks. "They're mating," replies her dad. "What do you call the spider on top, Daddy?" asks Lucy. "That's a daddy longlegs," he answers. Lucy continues, "So if that one's a daddy longlegs, the other must be a mommy lon-glegs?" "No, dear," says her daddy. "Both of them are daddy longlegs." Lucy thinks for a moment then stamps the insects flat. "Well," she says. "We're certainly not having THAT sort of thing in our garden!"

•••••

Robert, a college student, is talking to a friend. "Y'know," he says. "I think my roommate is queer." "Why d'you say that?" asks the friend. "Well," replies Robert. "Every time I kiss him goodnight, he shuts his eyes!"

•••••

Three gay men die in a car accident. All three are cre-mated. After the funeral their lovers discuss what will become of their ashes. The first man says, "My Jason was a pilot. He loved to fly, so I'm going up in a plane to scatter his ashes in the air!" The second man says, "My Rupert was a sailor. He just loved the water. I'm going to sail in a boat to scatter his ashes in the ocean!" The third man says, "Well, my Sammy was a great lover. He just loved to screw. I'm going to mix his ashes into a tub of chili powder and eat it. That way he can wreck my asshole just one last time!"

•••••

Two condoms stroll past a gay bar. One of them says, "Let's go in and get shit-faced!"

•••••

Two gay guys are on the beach. The first one says, "Shall I put the umbrella up?" "Well, okay," replies the second. "But don't open it—I'm still a bit sore!"

•••••

One morning Billy goes into the kitchen and finds his boyfriend, Jack, masturbating into a paper bag. "What on earth are you up to?" asks Billy. Jack replies, "I'm packing your lunch!"

•••••

Two gay men are walking down the street when one says, "You're not going to believe this, but I think I can smell a penis." The other replies, "Sorry, I just burped!"

•••••

What do a gay man and a bungee jumper have in common? If the rubber breaks they're both in deep shit!

What do a gay man and an ambulance have in common? They both get loaded from the rear and go, "Whoo! Whoo! Whoo...!"

What do you call a gay dentist? The tooth fairy!

What do you call a gay milkman? A dairy queen!

What do you call a homosexual dinosaur? A megasorass!

Three gay guys attacked a woman the other day. Two of them held her down while the other did her hair!

What's the quickest way to empty the men's restroom? Shout, "Nice dick!"

What's the difference between a gay man and a refrigerator? A refrigerator doesn't fart when you pull the meat out!

What's a homosexual masochist? A sucker for punishment!

What's the best gay pick-up line? "Can I push your stool in?"

Why did the gay guy think his lover was cheating on him? He came home shit-faced!

Why is the parking so good in San Francisco? Because no one dares to bend over long enough to paint the double yellow lines!

•••••

Brad comes home from work and greets his boyfriend, Stan. "Oh, Stan," says Brad. "All day I've had this feeling like I've got something stuck up my backside. Would you do me a favor and check it out for me." So Stan lubricates his finger and sticks it up Brad's ass and has a good feel around. "Nope—I can't feel anything," says Stan. "I'm sure there's something there," says Brad. "Maybe it's farther up. Try sticking your whole hand in." So Stan applies more lubricant and sticks his whole hand up Brad's backside. "Oh! Oh, wait a minute!" says Stan. "Yes! I think you're right—I can feel something up here." And Stan stretches and manages to reach the object and pull it out. "Holy crap!" he says. "I can't believe it! You had a Rolex watch up there." And Brad turns beaming to him and starts singing, "Happy birthday to you, happy birthday to you..."

•••••

Three gay men are sitting together in a hot tub. Suddenly a blob of semen floats to the surface of the water. They all look at each other. "Okay," says one. "Who farted?"

Gifts

A girl is talking to her friend, "My boyfriend bought me flowers for Valentine's Day," she says. "I guess that means spending the weekend with my legs in the air." "Why?" her friend asks. "Don't you have a vase?"

•••••

A wealthy woman is discussing Christmas presents with her maid. "Now what gift should I get the butler?" asks the woman. "A set of wine glasses?" suggests the maid. The woman frowns. "He doesn't need that—a butler never entertains. He'll get a tie. Now what about the cook?" The maid replies, "Why not get her a dress?" The woman frowns again, "She doesn't need a new dress—we'll get her another apron." "Now," says the woman. "What about my husband?" "I assume you want to get him something he really needs, madam?" asks the maid. "Of course," says the woman. The maid replies, "Then how about five more inches?"

God

Why did God create lesbians? So feminists couldn't breed!

Why did God create man? Because a vibrator can't mow the lawn!

Why did God give women nipples? To make suckers out of men!

Why did God invent yeast infections? So women know what it feels like to live with an irritating cunt!

How do we know God is a man? If God were a woman she'd have made sperm taste like chocolate!

Golf

Janet, a physiotherapist, tees off on the golf course but she slices her shot and hits a man standing on the next green. The man collapses, screaming, with his hand between his legs. Janet runs over and says, "Don't worry, I have medical training—I can help reduce the pain." As she says this, she opens his pants and massages his privates. After a minutes Janet asks, "Does that feel better?" The man replies, "Why, yes—thank you. But I think you broke my thumb!"

•••••

A man and his wife consult a golf pro to try and improve their game. The pro examines the man's technique and comments, "Your grip's too tight—imagine you're holding the club like you'd hold your wife's breasts." The man does so and hits the ball right onto the green. The next, the pro looks at the wife's technique. "I can see your problem," says the pro. "Your grip is too tight—handle the club as if it was your husband's penis." The woman does so, but only manages to knock the ball a few feet from the tee. "Okay," says the pro, "Not to worry. Now the first thing you have to do is take the club out of your mouth..."

•••••

George is at his golf club when he meets up with a new lady member. They start chatting and arrange to play a round. The lady turns out to be an excellent player and easily beats George. But there are no hard feelings and George takes her out for dinner. He then drives her home. One thing leads to another and she ends up giving George a blow job in his car. The same thing happens on four Sundays in a row until George suggests they go away for a dirty weekend. At this point the woman bursts into tears and confesses he's actually a transvestite. "What!" shouts George, "You rotten cheat! You've been playing off the ladies' tee for a whole month!"

●●●●●

On the day of their wedding, a groom makes his bride promise never to look in the top drawer of his desk. She agrees and twenty-five years pass before curiosity overcomes her and she has a peek inside. In the desk she's surprised to find three golf balls and a huge pile of cash. Later that day she confronts her husband and demands to know what's going on. "I'll confess," he says. "Every time I've had an affair I've put a golf ball in the desk." "You've had three affairs!" the wife exclaims, "Well, I'm not happy, but after twenty-five years I suppose I can live with it. Now tell me, where did all that money come from?" "Well," replies the husband. "Every time I collected a dozen balls, I sold them!"

Good Trick If You Can Do It

A guy walks into a bar and the bartender says, "See that horse over there? If you can make it laugh, you can have free drinks for the rest of the night." The man walks over to the horse, whispers something in the horse's ear and makes it laugh, so the bartender gives him his free drinks. The next night the guy comes back in and the bartender says, "If you can make that horse over there cry, I'll give you free drinks for a whole week." So the man walks over to the horse, drops his pants and the horse starts crying. The bartender is astonished and asks, "How did you make the horse do that?" The man replies, "Well, to make him laugh, I told him I had a bigger dick than him. And to make him cry—I showed him!"

•••••

A man is sitting on a train opposite a busty blonde wearing a tight mini skirt. Suddenly he realizes she's not wearing underwear. "Are you looking at my pussy?" asks the blonde. "I'm sorry," says the man, blushing. "That's all right," replies the woman, "I'm proud of my pussy. It's very talented. Watch this, I'll make it blow a kiss." And, sure enough, the blonde hitches up her skirt and her pussy blows the man a kiss. "I can make it wink, too," says the woman. The man stares in amazement as the pussy winks at him. "Why not come and sit next to me," says the blonde. So the man moves over. "Would you like to stick a couple of fingers up there?" asks the blonde. "Holy crap!" exclaims the man. "Y'mean, it can whistle as well?"

•••••

A man walks into a rough New Orleans bar with an alligator. "Who wants to see a cool trick?" he asks and then proceeds to stuff his genitals into the alligator's mouth. "Now how about this!" he shouts, then starts hitting the alligator over the head with a stick. The alligator is extremely annoyed by this, but refrains from biting the man and everyone is astonished when he finally pulls out his genitals without a scratch on them. "Anyone else got the guts to try it?" shouts the man. "Sure!" shouts a little old lady, "But don't hit me so hard with the stick!"

Gynecology

What do a gynecologist and a pizza delivery boy have in common? They can both smell it, but they can't eat it!

•••••

A woman goes to a gynecologist with an unusual problem: She has $1,000 stuck up her vagina. "I was in a bank that was being robbed," she explains. "They were taking everyone's money, but I managed to hide in a corner while I stuck my cash up my pussy. The trouble is, now I can't get it out!" "Not to worry," says the doctor. "Let me get you into the stirrups and I'll take a look." The woman takes off her underwear and lifts her legs while the doctor has a quick look inside her with a flashlight. The doctor goes quiet for a moment, then asks, "Look—before I go in there... What exactly am I looking for? $1,000 in bills or loose change?"

•••••

A young girl goes to a gynecologist for a checkup. The doctor puts her legs in the stirrups and notices that the girl is very nervous. "Is this your first time?" he asks. The girl nods. "Well, these instruments can be a little uncomfortable," says the doctor. "Would it help if I numbed you down there?" The girl nods gratefully. So the doctor buries his face between her legs and goes, "Numb, numb, numb, numb..."

Highly Sexed

A doctor tells his patient that after a long and active sex life his penis is burnt out and he can only use it another thirty times. The man goes home and tells his wife the bad news. "That's terrible," she says. "With so few left, we can't waste any. Let's make a list of special occasions." "Sorry," replies the man. "I already made a list—you're not on it!"

• • • • •

How can you tell if your girlfriend is horny? When you put your hand down her pants, it feels like you're feeding a horse!

• • • • •

A newly married couple are constantly having sex. When the husband comes downstairs in the morning, the wife asks what he'd like for breakfast. He replies, "I'll have sex, please!" So they go upstairs for sex and then he goes to work. When the husband comes home for lunch, his wife asks, "What would you like for lunch, dear?" He replies, "I'll have sex please!" So again they have sex and he returns to work. That evening he walks in the house and finds his wife sliding up and down the banister. "What are you doing?" he asks. She replies, "I'm warming up your dinner!"

•••••

I think you'll find that any of my girlfriends will tell you I'm a "five times a night man." I really shouldn't drink so much tea before I go to bed!

History

Did you hear about the perverted archaeologist? He could sniff a used tampon and tell you what period it was from!

•••••

For millions of years Neanderthal man was not fully erect… but then again Neanderthal women were real dogs.

•••••

A knight goes off on the Crusades, but to defend his wife's honor he equips her with a chastity belt embedded with razor blades. A year later he returns and orders all his retainers to drop their pants. They do so and the knight sees that all but one man have shredded privates. He stands before the unshredded man and says, "For your loyalty I shall give you my best horse and one hundred acres of land." The man replies, "Oh, hank u ery uch!"

•••••

Why did early men learn to walk upright? They wanted to leave their hands free for masturbation!

Hospitals and Operations

A doctor is doing the rounds of a maternity ward. "And when is Mrs. Smith due?" he asks the nurse. "The 5th of September," she replies. "I see," says the doctor. "And how about Mrs. Jones?" "She's due on the 5th, too," the nurse replies. "And Mrs. Evans?" asks the doctor. "She's also due on the 5th," says the nurse. "And—don't tell me—Mrs. Brown is due on the 5th as well," says the doctor. "I don't think so," replies the nurse. "She didn't go on the church picnic!"

• • • • •

A man is lying in a hospital bed with an oxygen mask over his face. A young nurse arrives to sponge his hands and feet. "Nurse," he mumbles from behind the mask, "Are my testicles black?" Embarrassed, the young nurse replies, "I don't know, I'm only here to wash your hands and feet." Again the man struggles to ask, "Nurse, are my testicles black?" "I'm sure I really don't know," stammers the nurse. Weakly, the man asks again, "But Nurse, are my testicles black?" The nurse gives in. She pulls back the covers, raises the man's gown, lifts the man's penis and takes a close look. "No, there's nothing wrong with them," she replies. The man rolls his eyes, pulls off his oxygen mask and says, "That was very nice but, *are my test results back?*"

• • • • •

A man's wife goes into a coma. One day a doctor calls the man and says that the nurses have seen signs of response from his wife when they wash her breasts. The man goes to the hospital, where the doctor suggests he try rubbing his wife's breasts himself. The man does so and there are definite signs of awareness from the woman. The next, the doctor suggests the man massages his wife's privates. He does so and the signs of awareness are even stronger. Finally, the doctor suggests something even more stimulating—oral sex. The man agrees and goes into his wife's room. Five minutes later the wife's heart monitor goes haywire. The doctor runs in. "My God!" he says. "What happened?" The husband replies, "I don't know—I think she choked!"

· · · · ·

A surgeon is operating on a man when he slips up and accidentally cuts off the man's testicles. To hide his mistake the surgeon slips an onion into the man's scrotum and sews it up. A month later the man comes back for a checkup. "So, have you noticed any differences since your operation?" asks the surgeon nervously. "A few," replies the man. "I cry when I pee, my wife gets heartburn if she gives me a blow job and I get an erection every time I go near a hot-dog stand!"

· · · · ·

How can you identify the head nurse in a hospital? She's the one with the dirty knees!

· · · · ·

The Queen is visiting one of Canada's top hospitals. During her tour she passes a room where a male patient is masturbating. The doctor accompanying her hurriedly explains. "I'm sorry, Your Highness," he says. "But this man has a serious condition where the testicles rapidly fill with semen. If he doesn't do that five times a day, they will explode." On the next floor they pass a room where a young nurse is giving a patient a blow job. "And what exactly is the problem with this gentleman?" asks the Queen. The doctor replies, "Same problem; better health plan!"

•••••

What's the worst part about getting a lung transplant? The first couple of times you cough, it's not your phlegm!

Hotels

A young couple walk into a hotel. "We'd like a room, please," says the man. "My wife and I were just married this morning." "Congratulations," says the desk clerk, "Would you like the bridal?" "No, thanks," replies the husband. "I'll hold her by the ears until she gets the hang of it!"

•••••

Jack checks into a simple country guesthouse for an overnight stay. The next morning he's getting packed when he finds he's desperate for a crap. Unfortunately his room doesn't have its own bathroom and the bathrooms in the hallway are occupied. He can't wait, so he's forced to crouch on the floor over a sheet of newspaper. Now Jack has the problem of hiding a huge smelly turd. He looks around and notices a large potted plant in the corner of his room. He lifts the plant out of the pot, drops in the turd and pushes the plant down on top of it. Phew! He's in the clear. A week later Jack is back home when he gets a letter from the guesthouse. The letter reads, "We know what you did. All is forgiven. But PLEASE tell us where you hid it!"

Hunting

A hunter goes out looking for buffalo and hires an Indian scout to help him. After a while the Indian gets off his horse, puts his ear to the ground and says, "Buffalo come." The hunter scans the area with his binoculars. "I can't see anything," he says. "How can you tell?" The Indian replies, "Ear sticky!"

• • • • •

Billy-Bob goes into the hills to hunt bears. He sees a huge grizzly, takes aim and misses. The bear runs up to him and asks, "Were you trying to kill me?" Billy-Bob nods. "Okay," says the bear. "This is how it works. If you try to kill me and fail I have the right to have sex with you. Now bend over and drop your pants." Billy-Bob does so and, half an hour later, he shuffles home with a sore bottom. The next day Billy-Bob returns with his gun. He sees a grizzly, shoots and misses. The bear runs over and asks, "Weren't you here yesterday?" Billy-Bob nods. The bear says, "Well, you know the drill. Bend over." The next day Billy-Bob returns. He sees a grizzly, shoots and misses. The bear comes over and asks, "You again?" Billy-Bob nods. "Y'know," says the bear. "I don't think you're really here for the hunting, are you…"

• • • • •

Three hunters are sitting around a campfire exchanging their worst experiences. The first guy says he was once up a ladder washing windows when the ladder collapsed and he broke every bone in his body. The second guy says he was hitchhiking once when a Greyhound bus ran over him, breaking his back. The third guy says, "Well, I'll tell you the *second* worst experience I ever had. One time I was out hunting and I had to take a crap, so I stepped behind a tree, dropped my pants and crouched. Then wham! A bear trap snapped shut on my testicles!" "Wow!" says the first guy. "If that was your second worst experience, what was the worst?" The third guy replies, "Well, that would be when I reached the end of the chain…"

Immigration

Two families move from Pakistan to the United States and the fathers make a bet to see which of them can become the most American in twelve months. A year later they meet up and the first man says, "Look at me. I am real American now. My son is playing quarterback, I am having a McDonalds breakfast and I am now on my way to the ball-park to root for my team. How about you?" The other man looks at him and says, "Fuck you, towel-head!"

Impotence

A man goes to the doctor complaining of impotence. The doctor examines him and says, "I can restore your sex drive, but it will require surgery. I can do it in a series of operations over a month that will cost $12,000, or I can do it in one operation right away that will cost $30,000 dollars. I suggest you go home and discuss the options with your wife." The next day the man calls up and announces, "We're going to redo the kitchen."

•••••

A man has his impotence cured with an elephant muscle transplant that increases the strength of his erections. On his first day out of the hospital he takes his girlfriend to dinner. The meal is going well until the man starts to feel aroused. At this point his fly bursts open and his huge new penis snakes out of his pants, grabs a bread roll and disappears under the table. "Wow!" says his girlfriend. "Can I see that again later in the bedroom?" "I don't know," the man replies. "There must be a limit to the number of bread rolls it can stuff up my ass!"

•••••

A wife is distraught because her husband's "little soldier" can't salute any more. She goes to her doctor and explains the situation. The doctor thinks for a while, then says, "Listen, I don't do this for everyone, but get this prescription and put three drops in his milk before he goes to bed." Two weeks later, the woman returns and the doctor asks how it went. "He's dead," sniffs the women. "I put thirty drops in his milk by accident. Now we're looking for an antidote so we can close the coffin!"

•••••

A woman goes to her doctor complaining that her husband is 300% impotent. "I'm not sure I know what you mean," says the doctor. "He's 300% useless!" replies the woman.

"He can't use his dick, he's got arthritis in his fingers and last week he burned his tongue!"

•••••

After fifteen years of marriage a woman discovers that her husband is impotent. In fact, all their married life he's been penetrating her with a strap-on rubber dildo. "That's awful," says his wife. "How could you deceive me like that?" "Gee, I'm sorry about the dildo," replies her husband. "But, y'know, I'm kind of interested in hearing your explanation for our three kids!"

•••••

After many years of married life a man discovers he's impotent. After seeking help everywhere he eventually turns to a witchdoctor. The witchdoctor casts a powerful spell and tells the man that all he has to do to get an erection is to recite, "One, two, three." He'll then be stiff for as long as he wants. To make the erection disappear, someone has to recite, "One, two, three, four." There's a catch, however: Once the spell has been used, it cannot be used again for another year. The man rushes home, gets into bed with his wife and says, "One, two, three." His puzzled wife replies, "What did you say, 'One, two, three' for?"

Impotence: Euphemisms for Impotence

Ascension Deficit Disorder.
Disappointing Miss Daisy.

Not rising to the level of impeachable offense.
Performing with Flaccido Domingo.
Serving boneless pork.
Taking the gold at the Lake Flaccid Olympics.
The Null Monty.
Unleavened Man-Bread.
Welcome to Flaccid City. Population: You.
180 degrees shy of heaven.

Infection

A guy and a girl are having sex. The girl asks, "You don't have AIDS, do you?" "No," the guy replies. "Oh, thank God!" she says. "I don't want to catch *that* again!"

•••••

A man goes to his doctor with an orange penis. "That's amazing," says the doctor. "Do you work with dyes or other chemicals?" "No," replies the man. "Do you have any unusual hobbies?" asks the doctor. "No," says the man. "So what do you do?" asks the doctor. "Well," replies the man. "Mostly I sit on the sofa watching porn and eating cheesy puffs!"

•••••

A man picks up a nasty infection in his penis and goes to a doctor. "I'm sorry," says the doctor. "I can't cure it. We're going to have to amputate." The man is horrified and goes to get a second opinion. "I'm sorry," says the second doctor.

"But your penis has got to come off." The man can't accept this and seeks a third opinion. "There's good news and bad news," says the third doctor. "The good news is that we don't have to cut off your penis." "And what's the bad news?" asks the man. The doctor replies, "It just came off in my hand!"

• • • • •

Doctor: "Your wife either has Alzheimer's or AIDS." **Husband:** "How can we find out which?" **Doctor:** "Drive her to the park and leave her there. If she finds her way home, don't fuck her!"

• • • • •

Two men are sitting in a doctor's waiting room. One says to the other, "What are you here for?" The other man replies, "I have a red ring around my dick. What are you here for?" He answers, "I've got a ring round my dick too, but mine is green." The doctor calls in the man with the red ring first. After the examination he walks the man out, telling him the red ring is no problem. He then invites the green ring man into his office. The man drops his pants. The doctor takes one look and says, "Bad news, I'm afraid. Your penis is going to fall off." "What?" he exclaims. "You told that guy with the red ring he was going to be okay!" "Well, yes," the doctor replies. "But there's a huge difference between lipstick and gangrene!"

• • • • •

Well, you know what they say, unlucky in love—get syphilis!

Innocence

A little boy goes to his mother and says, "Ma, every night I hear you and Pa making noises and when I look in your room you're bouncing up and down on him." His mother thinks quickly and says, "Oh, well, I'm bouncing on your father's tummy because he's fat and that makes him thin again." The boy says, "Well, that's not going to work." "Why not?" his mother asks. The boy replies, "Because the lady next door comes by every afternoon and blows him back up again!"

• • • • •

A little girl comes running into the house crying about a small cut on her finger. She asks her mother for a glass of cider. "Why do you want cider?" asks her mother. "To take the pain away," sobs the little girl. Her mother pours her a glass of cider and the little girl puts her finger in it. "It doesn't work!" she yells. "Why did you think it would?" her mother asks. "I heard Auntie say so," the girl replies. "She said that whenever she gets a prick in her hand, she can't wait to get it in cider!"

• • • • •

A little girl goes up to her father and says, "Daddy, when my cat died, why did it lie on its back with its legs in the air?" Her dad replies, "Well, its legs were up like that to make it easier for Jesus to grab hold of him and pull him up to heaven." "Gosh!" cries the girl. "That means Mommy almost died this morning!" "What d'you mean?"

asks her dad. "Well," the girl replies. "When I looked into Mommy's room she was lying on the bed with her legs in the air shouting, "Jesus! Jesus! I'm coming!" and if it hadn't have been for the mailman holding her down, he would have got her!"

• • • • •

A religious man wants to find a pure wife, so he devises a test: When he's out on a date he'll get his dick out and see how the young lady responds. He reckons this will be a sure way of finding out how much they know about sex. On his next date the man suddenly whips out his dick out. "What's that?" he says. The shocked woman replies, "That's a cock." "You Jezebel!" replies the man. "If you were pure you wouldn't know what to call it." The next week he goes on a date with another woman and, again, whips out his dick at the appropriate moment. "What's that?" he asks. The blushing woman responds, "Well, I'd call it a penis." "Hah!" says the man. "If you were pure, you wouldn't know what it was, you harlot!" The man goes on yet another date, but this time when he whips out his dick, the woman just giggles. "What's that?" asks the man. The girl titters and says, "Well, I guess that's what my Mommy would call a 'pee-pee.' I don't know though, I haven't seen one before." This is good enough for the man so he marries her. On their wedding night his young bride asks to see his "pee-pee" again. "Look," he says. "Since you're a married woman now, you can stop calling it a 'pee-pee.' Call it a 'dick.'" "Oh, you big silly," says the bride. "That's not a dick—a dick is ten inches long, three inches wide and black!"

•••••

An Amish woman and her daughter are riding in a buggy one cold January day. The daughter says to the mother, "My hands are freezing." The mother replies, "Then put your hands between your legs—they'll soon warm up." The next day the daughter is riding in a buggy with her boyfriend. The boyfriend says, "My hands are freezing." "Put them between my legs," replies the daughter. "They'll soon warm up." The next day the boyfriend is driving in the buggy with the daughter again. "My nose is freezing cold," he says. The daughter replies, "Put it between my legs—it'll soon warm up." The next day the boyfriend is out driving with the daughter yet again. "My penis is frozen solid," he complains. The next day the daughter is back driving in the buggy with her mother. "Have you ever heard of a penis?" asks the daughter. Her mother replies, "Certainly. Why do you ask?" "No reason," replies the daughter. "It's just that they make one hell of a mess when they thaw out!"

•••••

John and Mary were high school sweethearts who never had sex. "We'll wait till we're married!" insisted Mary. So John waits, and waits, and waits until finally, after a five-year engagement, they get married. On their wedding night Mary comes out of the bathroom and says, "I have some bad news. It's my time of the month so we'll have to wait a bit longer." She then gets into bed and goes to sleep. In the middle of the night she wakes up and she notices that John is wide awake glaring at the ceiling. "It's no use, John," says Mary. "We can't help it. You might as well get some rest!" "I wish I could," replies John, "but my dick is so hard, there's not enough skin left to close my eyes!"

•••••

To save money Jane and Tom have their honeymoon at the home of Jane's mother. Jane has never seen Tom naked before and is very nervous. When he takes off his shirt, she runs downstairs. "Mom," she says. "Tom has a hairy chest. Is that normal?" "Yes," her mother replies. "All good men have a hairy chest." Back upstairs Tom takes off his pants. Jane runs downstairs again. "Mom," she says. "Tom has hairy legs. Is that normal?" "Yes," replies her mother. "All good men have hairy legs." Back upstairs Tom takes off his underwear. Jane runs downstairs and says, "Mom, Tom's thingy is over a foot long. Is that normal?" "No," her mother replies. "Now stay here—this sounds like a job for Mommy!"

Kiddies' Favorites

What's green, slimy and smells of pork? Kermit's middle finger!

What's red and blue with a long string? A smurfette with her period!

Why can't Miss Piggy count to 70? She gets a frog in her throat at 69!

Kissing

Our lips touched—then she crossed her legs and broke my glasses.

Ladies of Lesbia

An old cowboy goes to a bar and orders a drink. As he sits sipping his whisky, a young lady sits down beside him. "Are you a real cowboy?" she asks. He replies, "Well, I've spent my whole life on the ranch, herding horses, mending fences and branding cattle, so I guess I am." The woman says, "Well, I'm a lesbian. I spend my whole day thinking about women. As soon as I get up in the morning, I think about women. When I shower, watch TV or eat, I think of women. In fact, everything seems to make me think of women." The woman finishes her drink and leaves. A little while later a man sits down next to the old cowboy. "Are you a real cowboy?" asks the man. The cowboy replies, "Well, I always thought I was, but I just found out I'm a lesbian!"

• • • • •

How can you spot the butch lesbian? She's the one that kick-starts her vibrator and rolls her own tampons.

What did the first lesbian say to the second lesbian? Your face or mine?

What do lesbians do after they have an argument? They go home and lick each other's wounds!

What do you call a cupboard full of lesbians? A licker cabinet.

What do you call a lesbian dinosaur? Lickalotopuss.

What do you call a lesbian with thick fingers? Well hung!

What do you call a Pakistani lesbian? Fadjeeta!

What do you call lesbian twins? Lick-a-likes.

What do you call two lesbians in a canoe? Fur traders.

What do you say to a butch lesbian with no arms and no legs? "Hi there, cutie pie. Nice tits!"

What's the definition of frenzy? Two blind lesbians walking through a fish market!

What's the leading cause of death for lesbians? Hair balls.

What's the politically correct name for a lesbian? A vagitarian!

Why do lesbians want to be reincarnated as whales? So they can have 12-foot long tongues and breathe out of the tops of their heads.

Laundry

A shy young couple invent a name for making love—"doing the laundry." One night the husband wakes up and asks his wife if she wants to "do the laundry." She complains that she's got a headache so the husband goes back to sleep. In the morning he again asks if she'd like to "do the laundry," but his wife complains she's too tired, after having a restless night. That afternoon he asks if she's ready to "do the laundry," but she's too busy with her chores. The same evening his wife snuggles up to him and asks if he still wants to "do the laundry." "No, it's okay," he replies. "It was a small load, so I did it by hand!"

•••••

A woman goes into a noisy launderette and asks the clerk for a service wash. "What!" the assistant shouts. "Come again?" "No!" shouts back the woman. "This time it's mustard!"

Laziness

A man sits in his garden reading a paper and drinking a beer while his wife struggles to push a mower across the lawn. A neighbor looks over the fence and comments, "It's a disgrace making your wife work like that while you laze about! You ought to be awfully well hung!" "I am," replies the man. "That's why she does all the work!"

Lepers

A leper walks into a bar and sits down. The bartender glances over and promptly vomits. The leper looks hurt. "Hey," he says. "I know I'm not exactly handsome, but I *do* have feelings." The bartender wipes his mouth and says, "I'm sorry, it wasn't you—the guy sitting next to you is dipping his chips in your neck!"

•••••

Two leper lovers walked down the road hand-in-hand, but they came back arm-in-arm!

Life in Remote Parts

A lumberjack goes to a remote logging station where there are no women for 500 miles. He asks his foreman what the locals do for sex. "Well, if you're feeling lonesome, Old Charlie will put you right. He's past sixty, but he can show you a good time." "Hell no!" cries the lumberjack. "I think I can do without Old Charlie!" However, six months later the lumberjack changes his mind. "Look," he says to the foreman. "How much does this Old Charlie charge?" "Three hundred and fifty dollars," replies the foreman. "Holy smoke!" says the lumberjack. "How comes he's so expensive?" "Well, Charlie only gets fifty dollars," replies the foreman. "But you have to pay three guys a hundred bucks each to hold him down!"

•••••

A prospector goes to a remote mining community and is horrified to find there are no women. He's even more shocked when he discovers that the locals use sheep for sex. For months the man resists temptation until he can't stand it any more. One night he goes out, finds a pretty young sheep and takes it to bed. The next day he decides to show off his new girlfriend and takes her to the town saloon. As soon as he enters the saloon with the ewe, the place goes silent and everyone stares at him in horror. "What's the matter with you all?" cries the man. "You all do it, so don't pretend you don't!" "Sure we do it," replies the bartender. "But never with the preacher's wife!"

Linguistics

A little boy goes up to his father. "Dad," he says. "What's the difference between 'potentially' and 'realistically'?" His father replies, "Well, go and ask your mother if she'd sleep with Robert Redford for a million dollars. Then ask your sister if she'd sleep with Brad Pitt for a million dollars. Then ask your brother if he'd sleep with Tom Cruise for a million dollars." So the boy asks these questions and each time the answer is, "Yes!" The boy goes up to his father and says, "I think I get it… Potentially we're sitting on three million dollars, but realistically we're living with two sluts and a fag!"

•••••

Little Johnny hears two new words, "bitch" and "pussy," and asks his Daddy what they mean. His father gets out a copy of *Playboy* and finds the centerfold. He then draws a circle round the model's crotch. "That's a pussy," he says. Johnny replies, "So what's a bitch?" Dad replies, "Everything out of the circle!"

Lion Taming

A circus owner advertises for a lion tamer. Two people show up, one is a young man and the other is a gorgeous girl. The circus owner says, "I'm not going to lie to you. This is a ferocious lion—he ate my last tamer, so you guys better be good. Here's your equipment: a chair, a whip and a gun. Who wants to try out first?" The girl volunteers to go first. She ignores the whip and the gun, steps into the lion's cage and sits in the chair. The lion charges, but the girl throws open her coat, revealing that she's naked underneath. The lion stops dead in his tracks, licks her all over, then rests its head in her lap. The circus owner is astonished. "I've never seen any thing like that in my life!" he shouts. He turns to the young man and asks, "Can you do that?" The young man replies, "Sure I can—as soon as you get that damn lion out of the way!"

Little Johnny

A few months after his parents' divorce, Little Johnny passes his mother's bedroom and sees her rubbing her body and moaning, "Oh… I need a man, I need a man!" Over the next couple of months, he sees her doing this several times. One day, he comes home from school and hears her moaning. He peeks into her bedroom and sees a man on top of her. Little Johnny runs into his room, tears off his clothes and starts stroking himself, "Oh… I need a bike… I need a bike!"

•••••

Little Johnny goes to school wearing a brand new watch. His best friend Benny asks how he got it. "Yesterday I got home early," says Johnny. "And I heard noises coming from my parents' bedroom. I walked in and saw Dad and Auntie Julie bouncing in bed. Dad said I could have anything I wanted as long as I didn't tell Mommy, so I asked for a watch." Benny decides he wants a watch too, so that night he listens outside his parents' bedroom. Eventually he hears some moaning and groaning, so he walks in and catches his parents in the act. Dad asks him what he wants. "I want a watch," says Benny. "Okay," replies his Dad. "You can stand in the corner, but don't make any noise!"

•••••

Little Johnny goes to stay on his uncle's farm. One morning his aunt tells him to feed the animals, but Little Johnny is in a bad mood. He kicks at the chickens when he scatters their corn. He kicks the cow when he gives it its hay. And he kicks the pig when he fills its trough. "I saw what you did," says his Aunt when he comes inside. "For kicking that chicken, you'll get no eggs this morning. For kicking the cow, you'll get no milk. And for kicking the pig, you'll get no bacon." At that moment his uncle comes in and kicks the cat away from his chair. Little Johnny looks at his aunt and says, "So, are you going to tell him, or shall I?"

•••••

Little Johnny goes up to his mother and says, "Is it true that babies come from storks?" "Why, yes," his mother replies. "Okay," says Johnny, "So who fucks the stork?"

•••••

At the public swimming pool the lifeguard approaches Little Johnny. "You're not allowed to pee in the pool," says the lifeguard. "I'm going to report you." "But everyone pees in the pool," Little Johnny replies. "Maybe," says the lifeguard. "But not from the diving board!"

•••••

Little Johnny is in class doing math problems. The teacher asks him a question. "Johnny," she says. "If there were four birds sitting on a fence and you shot one with your gun, how many would be left?" "None," replies Johnny. "If I shot one, the rest would fly away." "Well, that's not the answer I was looking for," says teacher. "But I like the way you're thinking." "Now I've got a riddle for you, miss," replies Little Johnny. "If you saw three women eating ice cream cones, and one was licking her cone, and one was biting her cone, and one was sucking her cone, how would you know which lady is married?" "Well," says the puzzled teacher, "I guess it would be the one sucking her cone?" "No," says Little Johnny, "It'd be the one wearing a wedding ring—but I like the way you're thinking!"

•••••

Little Johnny is in love with his pretty new kindergarten teacher. After class he goes up to her and asks her to marry him. "Why, Johnny," says the young woman. "How sweet of you. I would like to get married someday, but I'm not sure you're old enough; I don't want a child." Little Johnny replies, "Sure I'm old enough, and we can always use a rubber!"

•••••

Little Johnny is out walking with his mother when they see two birds mating. He asks what they're doing and his mother, embarrassed, tells him they're making sandwiches. A little while later they see two dogs mating. Again, Little Johnny asks what they're up to and again, his mother tells him they're making sandwiches. That night Little Johnny hears strange noises coming from his parents' room. He bursts in and switches on the light. "Mommy!" he cries. "You were making sandwiches!" "No, I wasn't!" protests his mother. "Yes you were," says Johnny. "You've got mayonnaise all down your chin!"

• • • • •

Little Johnny is standing in front of the class reading out his homework assignment. "I had to write about something I saw that was unusual," starts Johnny. "And yesterday I was walking home from school when I saw these two greyhounds running after each other. One of the dogs stopped suddenly and the one behind it was going so fast it rammed its head right up the other's ass." "Johnny!" snaps the teacher. "We don't use the word 'ass' in this classroom; we say 'rectum.'" Johnny replies, "'Rectum?' Hell, it damn near killed 'em!"

• • • • •

Little Johnny passes his parents bedroom, where he sees them having sex. The next day he asks his mother why she was doing what he'd seen her do. "I was doing that because I want a baby," his mother replies. The next night Little Johnny sees his mother giving his father a blow job and the next day he asks her about it, "Were you doing that because you wanted another baby?" "No," replies his mother. "I was doing that because I want a BMW!"

• • • • •

Little Johnny passes his parents' bedroom in the middle of the night. Hearing a lot of moaning and thumping, he peeks in and catches his folks in the act. Before his father can react, Little Johnny shouts, "Oh, boy! Horsey ride! Daddy, can I ride on your back?" Daddy, relieved that Johnny's not asking uncomfortable questions, agrees. Johnny hops on and Daddy gets back into the rhythm.

Pretty soon Mommy starts moaning and gasping. Johnny cries out, "Hang on tight, Daddy! This is the part where me and the milkman usually get bucked off!"

•••••

Little Johnny runs into class half an hour late. "Sorry, miss," he says, "I'm late because I had to make my own breakfast." The teacher accepts this excuse, but as a punishment makes him stand up and answer some questions on geography. "Now, Johnny," says the teacher. "Tell me where the Canadian border is." "In bed screwing my mother," he replies. "Why do you think I had to make my own breakfast?"

•••••

Little Johnny runs into the bathroom and finds his mother taking a shower. "Mommy, what's that?" he asks, pointing at her crotch. "Er, that's… um… my bush," replies his mother. He then points at his mother's chest and asks, "And what are those?" "Those are… um… my flashlights," she replies. The next day the same thing happens, but it's Little Johnny's father in the shower. "Daddy, what's that?" asks Johnny, pointing at his father's crotch. "That's my… um… snake," his father replies. That night Johnny asks his parents if he can sleep in their bed. "Well, okay," his father says. "But only as long as you don't look under the covers." Little Johnny agrees, but he wakes up to hear strange noises and takes a peek under the sheets. "Mommy! Mommy!" he yells. "Quick, turn on your flashlight! Daddy's snake is going through your bush!"

• • • • •

Little Johnny runs up to his mother and says, "Mommy, why has Granny got a shrimp between her legs?" "Don't be silly—Granny doesn't have a shrimp there," his mother replies. Johnny is insistent. "She does, she *does*!" he shouts and drags his mother into his grandma's room. It's a very hot evening and Granny is in bed fast asleep, lying naked on top of her covers. Johnny points between Granny's legs. "Look, I told you so!" he shouts. "A little shrimp!" "That's not a shrimp," says his mother. "Oh, yeah?" says Johnny. "Well, it sure tastes like one!"

• • • • •

Little Johnny visits his uncle's farm and sees a bull mounting a cow. "Wow!" says Johnny. "Look at that bull fucking that cow!" "Don't use that word," scolds his uncle. "If you have to refer to that sort of behavior say that the bull is 'surprising' the cow." That evening Little Johnny and his uncle's family are sitting down to dinner. Johnny glances out of the window and says, "Holy smoke! That bull is really surprising those cows!" His uncle says, "You mean 'cow'—a bull can't surprise more than one cow at once." "Oh, yes, he can," replies Johnny. "They're watching him fuck that horse!"

• • • • •

Little Johnny walks past his parent's bedroom one day and sees his father sitting on the side of the bed sliding on a condom. His father realizes he's being watched and quickly slides over to the other side of the bed to hide his erection. "What's going on?" asks Johnny. "Oh," his father replies.

"Well, y'know, I thought I just saw a rat run under this bed."

"Wow!" says Johnny. "So what ya gonna do, fuck him?"

•••••

Little Johnny's mother walks by his room and sees him masturbating. Later she has a talk with him and tells him that good little boys save it until they are married. A few weeks later she asks him, "How are you doing with that problem we talked about, Johnny?" Little Johnny replies, "Great! So far I've saved nearly a quart!"

•••••

One night, Little Johnny's father overhears his son saying his prayers, "God bless Mommy, Daddy and Grandma. Goodbye Grampa." The next day his grandfather dies. A month or so later, his father again overhears Little Johnny at prayer: "God bless Mommy and Daddy. Goodbye, Grandma." The next day his grandmother dies. His father begins to worry. Two weeks later, he again hears Little Johnny praying, "God bless Mommy. Goodbye Daddy." His father nearly has a heart attack and spends all next day in fear of his life. However, he manages to survive and returns home after work. "I had a really bad day today," he says to his wife. "Don't tell me about bad days," his wife replies. "This morning the mailman dropped dead on the porch!"

•••••

A teacher asks her class to call out the names of things in alphabetical order. "What name begins with an A?" she asks. Little Johnny sticks up his hand, but his teacher ignores him. "He'd probably say something rude like

'Asshole,'" she thinks. Little Tommy is chosen and he says, "A is for Ant." "Now, what name begins with B?" asks the teacher. Little Johnny sticks up his hand, but his teacher ignores him again. "He'd only say something like 'Bitch,'" thinks the teacher. Little Suzie is chosen and she says, "B is for Bear." This goes on for ten minutes with all the children being given a chance to name something. The teacher gets to "R" and realizes that only Little Johnny has not yet had a turn. "He'll probably say 'Retard' or something," she thinks. However, it *is* Johnny's turn, so she braces herself for some profanity and picks him. "R is for Rat," says Johnny. "Oh," says the relieved teacher. "That's right, Johnny. Very good." "A big bad motherfucking rat," continues Johnny, "with a twelve-foot dick!"

• • • • •

A teacher asks her class to talk about something they think is important. Little Johnny sticks up his hand and is called to the front of the class. He draws a dot on the blackboard. "What's that?" asks the teacher. "It's a period," Johnny replies. "Well, that's very nice," says teacher. "But is it very important?" "Well, I guess it must be," Johnny replies. "This morning my sister said she'd missed hers, and Daddy had a heart attack, Mommy fainted and the man next door shot himself!"

Lubrication

A newlywed couple didn't know the difference between putty and Vaseline. A week after the marriage all their windows fell out… which was the least of their worries!

•••••

A woman goes into a drugstore with her three young children and starts browsing. "May I help you?" asks the salesclerk. "I need some Vaseline so I can make love with my husband," replies the woman. "After having three children I wouldn't have thought you'd need Vaseline," the assistant remarks. "That's exactly why I need it," she replies. "We put it on the bedroom doorknob so they can't get in!"

Magic, Myth and Fantasy

An attractive young woman is sunbathing in her back garden when she sees a little old man crouched in her flowerbed. She leaps on him and shouts, "You're a goblin! And now that I've caught you, you must give me three wishes! I want a big mansion, lots of money and a handsome prince to marry!" "Okay," says the little old man. "I can do all that, but for the magic to work you have to go to bed with me." The woman agrees and they spend the afternoon in the bedroom. After they've finished the little old man starts putting on his clothes. "I hope you don't mind me asking," he says. "But how old are you exactly?" "Twenty-two and a half," the woman replies. "Christ!" mutters the little old man. "Twenty-two, and she still believes in goblins."

•••••

A man goes up to a girl in a bar. "You want to play 'Magic'?" he asks. "How d'you play that?" she replies. "It's easy," says the man. "We go to my house and have sex… then you disappear!"

• • • • •

Mike is walking along one day when he comes across a magic beanstalk. Curious, he begins to climb and before long he finds the ugliest woman he's ever seen, sitting on a leaf. She beckons to him and says, "Have sex with me, or climb the beanstalk to success." Mike shudders and climbs higher. A bit farther on he comes across a very plain woman sitting on a leaf. "Have sex with me, or climb the beanstalk to success," she says. Again, Mike continues his climb. Before long, he comes upon another woman. This one is very attractive. "Have sex with me, or climb the ladder to success," she says. This time Mike is tempted but he figures that, if the women get better-looking the higher he climbs, he might as well keep going. Mike climbs higher and comes across a leaf right at the top of the beanstalk. Standing on the leaf is a huge dirty ugly old hillbilly wearing nothing but a pair of torn jeans. The old man undoes his buttons and his jeans fall around his ankles, leaving him naked. "Howdy," says the man. "Who the hell are you?" asks Mike. The man replies, "I'm Cess!"

• • • • •

The Seven Dwarfs visit Rome and are lucky enough to be granted an audience with the Pope. While they're talking, Dopey asks a question. "Excuse me, sir," he says. "But are there any dwarf nuns in the Vatican?" "No," the Pope replies. "There are not." "So are there *any* dwarf nuns in Rome?" asks Dopey. "No," says the Pope. "There are not." "So are there any dwarf nuns in the whole of Italy?" asks Dopey. The Pope thinks for a second, then says, "No, no there are not…"

And the other dwarfs start chanting, "Na-na na-na-na! Dopey screwed a penguin! Dopey screwed a penguin…!"

• • • • •

The Three Bears come back from a walk and see that the front door of their house is swinging open. Fearing they've been burgled, they run indoors and search the property. After going over the house from top to bottom they gather in the kitchen. "I'm sure someone's been here," says Mama Bear. "I know," says Papa Bear. "But nothing seems to be missing. Has anything of yours been taken, Baby Bear?" "No," Baby Bear replies. "But some-one's been through my closet and now the handle of my tennis racket smells like tuna!"

• • • • •

Thor, the Norse God of Thunder, gets bored of Valhalla and descends to Earth to get some action. He meets a girl in a bar and she takes him back to her place. Thor, having the stamina of a god, then has constant sex with the girl for fourteen hours. The next day, Thor is boasting to his fellow gods about his prowess, but Odin tells him off. "You can't submit human women to so much divine sex," he says. "They don't have the strength. You might have injured her. Go back to Earth, find this woman and apologize." So Thor goes back to the girl's apartment and knocks on the door. She shuffles to the door and opens it. "Look," he says. "Sorry about last night and everything—I ought to explain. You see, I'm Thor…" "Oh! So you're thor, are you?" com-plains the girl. "Poor you—I can't even *pith*!"

•••••

What did Cinderella do when she got to the ball? She choked!

•••••

What did the Seven Dwarves say when the handsome prince woke up Snow White? "Well, boys, I guess it's back to wanking!"

Mail

The mailman in a small town is about to retire. On his last day of work he goes to the first house on his route, and the homeowner gives him a bottle of bourbon. At the next house they give him $100, and at the third house he receives a huge cake. However, when he rings the bell at the fourth house the door is answered by a beautiful lady wearing a kimono. She takes him upstairs and gives him the best sex he's ever had, then takes him into the kitchen and makes him a huge breakfast. Finally, she hands him $5. "Wow!" says the mailman. "I've had the best day of my entire life. But I have to ask, what's the five bucks for?" "Well," the lady replies. "When I asked my husband what we should do for your retirement, he said, 'Fuck him! Give him five dollars,' but the breakfast was my idea!"

•••••

Three women are talking about their sex lives. One says, "I call my husband 'The Dentist' because nobody can drill like he does." The next says, "Well, I call my husband 'The Miner' because he has an incredible shaft." The third sighs and says, "I call mine 'The Postman.'" "Why 'Postman'?" asks the first. The woman replies, "Because he always delivers late and half the time it's in the wrong box!"

Marine Life

A woman vanishes in a boating accident. The next day the police tell her husband they have some bad news, some good news and some more good news. "The bad news is that we pulled your wife's body from the bottom of the lake," says one policeman. "Oh, my God!" cries the husband. "What's the good news?" "We pulled three big crabs and a king-size lobster off her," the policeman replies. "You call that good news?" exclaims the horrified husband. "What on earth was the other good news?" "We're pulling her up again tomorrow!" says the policeman.

•••••

A scuba diver gets arrested for having sex with a dolphin. His wife is furious. "How could you?" she says. "Caught making love to a dolphin! That's it, I'm leaving you." "Doesn't bother me," he says. "There's plenty more fish in the sea!"

•••••

Did you hear about the gay whale? He bit off the tip of a submarine and sucked out all the seamen!

•••••

A man walks into a jazz club with an octopus on his shoulder. "This octopus is a musical genius," he says. "I'll give

$100 to any person who can find a musical instrument my octopus can't play." A number of people give the octopus their instruments: a saxophone, a guitar, a harmonica, etc., but the octopus can play all of them. Eventually a Scotsman pushes his way through the crowd and hands the octopus a set of bagpipes. The octopus goes frantic and starts pulling the pipes all over the place, but without producing any music. "Ah!" cries the Scotsman. "I knew it! He canna' play the pipes." "Play it?" says the octopus. "Who wants to play it? As soon as I get its pajamas off, I'm going to fuck it!"

• • • • •

What do a walrus and Tupperware have in common? They both like a nice tight seal!

• • • • •

What's pink and drags along the ocean floor? Moby's dick!

Marital Aids

A woman goes to a doctor. It turns out she has a vibrator lodged inside her pussy. "Not a problem," says the doctor. "Get on the couch—I'll have it out in a jiffy." "Get it out?" exclaims the woman. "I don't want it out! I want you to change the batteries!"

• • • • •

A woman goes into an adult store to buy a dildo. The guy behind the counter shows her a few, but she doesn't like any of them. And so the guy says, "Well, we do have a special for $150. It's called the Magic Dildo. Whenever you say

'Magic Dildo my—something' it starts screwing you there."
Impressed, the woman buys the Magic Dildo and leaves.
While she's driving home she decides to try it out. "Magic
Dildo my shoulder!" says the woman, and it starts humping her shoulder. The next, she says, "Magic Dildo my
pussy!" and the dildo starts screwing her. Unfortunately it
works so well she can't control the car and it starts swerv-
ing over the road. A cop pulls her over and asks her what
she's doing. "I'm sorry, officer," she says. "But I just bought
a Magic Dildo and it was distracting me." The cop has
heard some wild excuses, but this one takes the cake.
"Yeah, right," he says. "Magic Dildo my ass!"

• • • • •

I tried some of that aphrodisiac rhino horn and it really
worked. I'm really beginning to like those rhinos now!

• • • • •

On the beach, how can you recognize a guy who uses an
inflatable sex doll? He doesn't stare at the bikinis—he stares
at the beach balls!

• • • • •

A little old lady totters into a sex shop. She shakily hobbles the few feet to the counter and grabs it for support.
"Ddddoooo yoouuu hhhave ddddddildossss?" she asks the
sales clerk. To which he replies, "Yes, we do have dildos."
The old lady says, "Ddddddooooo yyyouuuu hhhave aaaa
pppinkk onnne, ttttten inchessss llllong aaaaand aaaaabboutt
ttwwooo inchesss thhhththiiickkk?" The clerk replies, "Yes,
I believe we do." "Iiiiinnnn thaaaaat ccaaaassse," says the
little old lady, "Cccccoullddd yyyyouuu tellll mmmeeee

hhhowwww ttoooo ttturnn tthe ffffrigggingg thingggg offffffff?"

•••••

My husband came home with a tube of KY Jelly. "This will make you happy tonight, darling," he said. He was right. When he went to the bathroom, I squirted it all over the doorknob so he couldn't get back in!

Married Life

A man and his wife are having sex. Fifteen minutes pass, then thirty, then forty-five. Sweat is pouring off both of them. The wife finally looks up and says, "So what's the matter, darling? Can't you think of anyone?"

•••••

A man walks into a whorehouse and lays down $200. He says, "I want a girl that'll go to bed and just lay still!" The madame replies, "But sir, for $200 you could have the best girl in the house!" "No, thank you," the man replies. "I'm not horny, just homesick!"

•••••

What's the difference between a wife and jelly? Jelly moves when you eat it!

•••••

Two married friends are out drinking. One says to the other, "I can never sneak into the house after I've been out all night. I've tried everything. I turn the headlights off before I get to the driveway, I shut off the engine and coast into the garage, I take my shoes off and creep up the stairs… I get undressed in the bathroom, I do everything, but my wife still wakes up and yells at me for staying out so late." His friend replies, "Do what I do—I screech into the driveway, slam the front door, storm up the steps, throw my shoes into the closet, jump into bed, slap my wife's ass and say, 'How about a blow job?' and she always pretends she's asleep!"

•••••

The three stages of marital sex: Honeymoon sex—where you have sex three or four times a night; Vacation sex—where you have sex ten or twelve times a year; Oral sex—where you stand on the opposite side of the room and shout, "Fuck you!"

•••••

A husband and wife get into bed. The wife curls up ready for sleep and her husband puts on a lamp to read a book. He reads for a little while, then stops, reaches over to his wife, rubs her pussy, then starts reading again. His wife starts to undress. "What are you doing, darling?" asks the man. "Getting ready for sex," replies his wife. "I'm too tired for that," says the husband. "Then why were you rubbing my pussy?" his wife asks. "Oh *that*," replies the husband. "I was just wetting my finger to turn the pages!"

•••••

Last night my wife met me at the front door. She was wearing a sexy negligee. The only trouble was, she was coming home!

• • • • •

A man comes home from the night shift and goes to bed. He finds his wife under the sheets and makes love to her. After this activity he wants a snack and goes downstairs to the kitchen. He's amazed to find his wife reading a magazine. "What are you doing down here?" he asks. "We were just upstairs screwing!" "Oh, my God!" gasps his wife. "That was my mother in our bed! She came over and said she was feeling ill!" The wife runs upstairs to the bedroom. "Mother," she says. "I can't believe this. Why didn't you say something?" The mother snorts and says, "*What*? I haven't spoken to that moron in ten years—I'm not about to start now!"

• • • • •

A woman complains to her doctor about her husband's low sex drive and he gives her some "pep" pills to slip into his coffee. That weekend the wife slips a pill into her husband's coffee, but decides she might as well go for broke and tips in a dozen or so. On Monday the doctor calls to find out if the pills worked. The woman's son answers the phone, "Doc, thank God you called," he says. "I don't know what to do—Mom's dead, Grandma's passed out, my sister's in the hospital, my asshole hurts like hell and Dad's out on the porch, whistling for the dog!"

• • • • •

A woman says to her husband, "Y'know, I can still get into the same skirts I wore before we got married." The husband replies, "I sure wish I could!"

• • • • •

Always talk to your wife when you're making love— assuming there's a phone handy.

• • • • •

Two blondes are talking: "So what do you think our hus-bands talk about when they're out drinking?" says one. The other replies, "Probably the same things we talk about." The first blonde thinks for moment, then says, "Jesus! Those sick dirty bastards!"

• • • • •

Two men are having a drink. One says, "I had sex with my wife before we were married. What about you?" "I don't know," the other replies. "What was her maiden name?"

Massage

A man goes to a massage parlor for the first time and is invited to lie down on a couch. As the masseur kneads him she notices the man has developed an enormous erection. She bends over and whispers, "Would you like a hand job?" "Yes, please," he replies. The masseur slips out of the room. Five minutes later she sticks her head around the door and asks, "Have you finished?"

Masturbation

He's the world's greatest athlete. They held a masturba-tion contest and he finished first and third!

How did Pinocchio find out he was made of wood? When his hand caught fire!

I'm better at sex than anyone I know—now all I need is a partner!

Mothers have Mother's Day and fathers have Father's Day. What do single guys have? Palm Sunday!

•••••

Pinocchio gets a girlfriend, but she complains of getting splinters when they make love. He goes to his doctor for advice and is told to use a sheet of sandpaper. The next week the doctor sees Pinocchio in the street. "How's it going with the girlfriend?" asks the doctor. "Girlfriend?" says Pinocchio. "Who needs a girlfriend?"

•••••

To stop me from masturbating my father used to put something in my tea—my penis!

What's the definition of a Yankee? Same thing as a "quickie," but you do it yourself!

What's the ultimate rejection? When you're masturbating and your hand falls asleep!

When I was 12 my father told me that if I masturbated I'd go blind. I said, "I'm over here, Dad!"

When you're jacking off, what's the most sensitive part of your body? Your ears, listening out for footsteps!

Why do men like masturbation? It's sex with someone they love.

Why is masturbating like eating at McDonalds? Because it's always exactly the same and afterwards you swear you'll never do it again!

Why is sex like a game of poker? You don't need a partner if you've got a good hand!

Masturbation: Euphemisms for Male Masturbation

Adjusting the antenna.
Aiding and abetting a known felon.
Applying the hand brake.
Arm-wrestling the purple-headed storm-trooper.
Auditioning the hand puppet.
Banging the cyclops.
Beating the bishop.
Blowing your own trumpet.
Bludgeoning the beefcake.
Buffing the banana.
Burping the worm.
Checking Darth Vader's collar size.
Checking Prince Philip for mumps.
Choking Charlie till he pukes.
Choking Kojak.
Choking the chicken.
Competing at Onan's Olympics.
Dancing with Johnny One-Eye.
Digitally oscillating one's penis.
Doing one-handed tae kwan do.
Doing the Han Solo.
Doing the Jedi hand trick.
Doing the underarm javelin in the meat Olympics.
Double-clicking the mouse.

Downloading from your personal website.

Dusting the old trophy.

Enjoying a menage à moi.

Entertaining the emu.

Escorting the one-eyed postal worker out of his denim cell.

Evicting the testicular squatters.

Fastening the chin strap on the helmet of love.

Fixing the Hubble telescope.

Flogging the dolphin.

Flogging the log.

Fondling the figs.

Freeing the slaves.

Frosting the pastries.

Getting the boys ready for the play-offs.

Giving the carpet a midnight feast.

Going for the jackpot on the one-arm bandit.

Grooming the wookie.

Having a tug-of-war with the cyclops.

Helping put Mr. Kleenex's kids through college.

Helping the bald-headed hermit gargle.

Helping the python shed its skin.

Holding the sausage hostage.

Igniting the light saber.

Jerkin' the gherkin.

Juggling the javelin.

Juicing the moose.

Keeping the optometrists in business.

Launching a Jism Probe into the Tissue Nebula.

Launching the tadpoles.

Lighting the lava lamp.

Making a cash withdrawal.

Making the bald man puke.

Making the hooded cobra spit.

Mangling the midget.

Manipulating the mango.

Massaging the one-eyed monk.

Oiling the pogo stick.

Paddling the two-toned trouser trout.

Painting maps of Hawaii on your stomach.

Painting the ceiling.

Playing a solo on the single string air guitar.

Playing pocket billiards.

Playing the one-string banjo.

Playing the pink oboe.

Playing tug-of-war with the cyclops.

Polishing the crown jewels.

Polishing the lighthouse.

Pounding the pudding.

Pumping gas at self service island.

Punchin' the munchkin.

Putting the seminal luge team through their paces.

Putting your thumb in the porridge.

Releasing the hostages.

Releasing the Olympic doves.

Relishing your hot dog.

Roughing up the suspect.

Shaking hands with the unemployed.

Shellacking the shillelagh.

Shooting putty at the moon.

Slapping the purple-headed yogurt pistol.

Spanking the monkey.

Spanking the plank.

Strangling the midget.

Stroking the salami.

Summoning the genie.
Taking Herman to the circus.
Taming the beef weasel.
Teaching the cyclops the lambada.
Thumbing for a ride.
Tweaking the twinkie.
Twistin' the piston.
Unleashing the alabaster yak.
Unsheathing the meat saber.
Unwrapping the pepperoni.
Varnishing the banister.
Waxing the flagpole.
Whipping up some sour cream.
Wrangling the invertebrate serpent.
Wrestling with your emotions.
Yanking the yam.

Masturbation: Euphemisms for Female Masturbation

Auditioning the finger puppets.
Basting the tuna.
Beating the beaver.
Buffing the muff.
Buttering the muffin.
Checking for squirrels.
Checking the oil.
Cleaning between the camel's toes.
Clubbing the clam.
Dialing "O" on the little pink telephone.

Dunking the doughnut.

Excavating the Tunnel of Love.

Exercising the negotiator.

Exploring the bush.

Exploring the Deep South.

Flicking the switch.

Frosting the muffin of love.

Getting the last pickle out of the jar.

Glazing the doughnut.

Going on a self-guided boat tour through tuna country.

Groping the grotto.

Having a wander through no man's land.

Impeaching President Bush.

Itching the ditch.

Juicing the sluice.

Lathering up Old Mossyface.

Making panty pudding.

Making the kitty purr.

Mistressbation.

Moistening the oyster.

Parting the Red Sea.

Perusing the Yellow Pages.

Playing a solo on the fur-trimmed accordion.

Preheating the oven.

Rocking the little man in the boat.

Sending Muffin Morse Code.

Shaking the dew off the lily.

Slamming the clam.

Sorting the mail.

Stirring the cauldron.

Strumming the banjo.

Sweeping the chimney.
Testing the battery.
Testing the plumbing.
Tickling your fancy.
Tiptoeing through the two lips.
Unclogging the drain.
Unwrapping the gift box.
Worshiping nature's tufted treasure.

Men

Men are like snowstorms—you never know when they are coming, how many inches you'll get, or how long it will last!

•••••

Why do men find it hard to make eye contact? Boobs don't have eyes!

•••••

Why do men like big tits and tight pussy? Because they've got big mouths and little dicks!

•••••

Why do men name their penises? Because they like to be on a first-name basis with the one who makes all their decisions!

•••••

Why is it that when a man talks dirty to a women it's sexual harassment, but when a women talks dirty to a man, it's $3.99 a minute?

• • • • •

Why do men like having sex with the lights on? It makes it easier to put a name to the face!

• • • • •

He's such a chauvinist. He hates every bone in a woman's body, except his own!

• • • • •

Men are like trains—they always stop before you get off.

Military

Why is being in the military like a blow job? The closer you get to discharge, the better you feel.

• • • • •

A sergeant calls a surprise medical inspection on a group of Marines. He lines them up outside their barracks in three rows and then looks over each man before the doctor arrives. The sergeant sees a man in the back row scratching his arm, so he whacks the man's elbow with a stick. "Did that hurt, soldier?" he bellows. "No, sir!" comes the reply. "Why not?" the sergeant shouts. "Because I'm a Marine!" the soldier yells back. The sergeant then sees a man in the middle row rubbing his nose. He whacks the man over the head. "Did that hurt, soldier?" the sergeant bellows. "No, sir!" is the reply. "Why not?" the sergeant shouts. "Because I'm a Marine!" yells back the soldier. The sergeant then sees a man in the front row with a huge erection. The sergeant whacks the erection with his stick and bellows, "Did that hurt, soldier?" "No, sir!" he replies. "Why not?" the sergeant shouts. The soldier says, "Because it belongs to the man behind me!"

●●●●●

On the battlefield an officer orders a soldier to try and save a military warehouse that's been set on fire by the enemy. To get to a hose the soldier dodges bullets, wipes out a machine gun nest and blows up an enemy tank. On the way back he kills three men barehanded, shoots down an enemy helicopter and destroys an enemy base. He then climbs all over the burning building with his hose extinguishing every flame he can find. The officer salutes him. "That was the most heroic thing I ever saw," he says. "You'll get a medal for saving that warehouse." "Warehouse?" says the soldier. "Shit! I thought you said, 'whorehouse'!"

Milkman

A milkman knocks on Mrs. Smith's door to settle her bill. Mrs. Smith answers the door wearing a sexy nightie and suggests that she pays the $5 she owes along with having sex. The milkman agrees and they go to the bedroom. There, the milkman strips off and reveals he's got the biggest penis Mrs. Smith has ever seen. He then takes some large rubber washers out of his pocket and starts slipping them over the end of his monster. "There's no need for that," says Mrs. Smith. "It might be big, but I can take all of it." "Oh, yeah?" the milkman replies. "Not for a fuckin' fiver, you won't!"

Money

A husband and wife are trying to save for their vacation. The husband suggests that he puts a $20 bill in a jar every time they have sex. Three months later the man counts the money and finds over $800. "How did that happen?" asks the husband. "We only had sex six times." His wife replies, "Yeah, but not everyone's as tight-fisted as you are!"

• • • • •

A son from a poor family wins a million dollars in the lottery. He goes home and gives his old dad $100. The old man takes the cash and says, "Thanks, son. This money will mean a lot to me—we've never had much in this family; we've always been poor... I couldn't even afford to marry your mother." "What?" exclaims the son. "You mean, I'm a bastard?" "Yes," his father replies. "And a fucking cheap one, too!"

• • • • •

Why did the Irish call their currency the "punt"? Because it rhymes with "bank manager"!

Mommy, Mommy...

"Mommy, Mommy! Are you sure this is how to learn to swim?" "Shut up and get back in the sack!"

"Mommy, Mommy! Billy won't let go of my ear!" "Billy, let go of Susie's ear! Billy! Let go of her ear! All right, Billy, give me the ear!"

"Mommy, Mommy! Can I lick the bowl?" "No, flush it like everyone else!"

"Mommy, Mommy! Can I play in the sandbox?" "Not until I find a better place to bury Daddy!"

"Mommy, Mommy! Can I wear a bra now that I'm 16?" "Shut up, Albert!"

"Mommy, Mommy! Daddy's had a heart attack!" "Don't make me laugh, you know my lips are chapped."

"Mommy, Mommy! Daddy's on fire!" "Quick, grab a burger and a frying pan!"

"Mommy, Mommy! Grandma's going out!" "Well, throw on some more gasoline!"

"Mommy, Mommy! Grandma's got a big hairy wart!" "Shut up and eat around it!"

"Mommy, Mommy! I don't like bows in my hair!" "Shut up and lift the other arm!"

"Mommy, Mommy! I don't like running in circles!" "Shut up, or I'll nail your other foot to the floor!"

"Mommy, Mommy! I don't like this tomato soup!" "Shut up, we only have it once a month!"

"Mommy, Mommy! I don't wanna visit grandma!" "Shut up and keep digging!"

"Mommy, Mommy! I don't want hamburgers for supper!" "Shut up or I'll grind your other hand!"

"Mommy, Mommy! I don't want lemonade!" "Shut up and lift my skirt!"

"Mommy, Mommy! I don't want to see Niagara Falls!" "Shut up and get back in the barrel!"

"Mommy, Mommy! I hate my sister's guts!" "Shut up and eat what's put in front of you!"

"**Mommy, Mommy!** I want to play with Grandpa!" "Keep quiet—the coffin's staying closed!"

"**Mommy, Mommy!** I've lost my fingers!" "Shut up and eat your French fries!"

"**Mommy, Mommy!** My egg tastes bad!" "Stop complaining! Just eat it!" "But, Mommy, do I have to eat the beak as well?"

"**Mommy, Mommy!** My head hurts!" "Shut up and hold the dartboard still!"

"**Mommy, Mommy!** Sally won't come skipping with me!" "Shut up! You know it makes her stumps bleed!"

"**Mommy, Mommy!** What are you doing with that axe…?"

"**Mommy, Mommy!** What's a lesbian?" "Ask your father— she knows."

"**Mommy, Mommy!** What's a nymphomaniac?" "Shut up and help me get Grandma off the doorknob!"

"**Mommy, Mommy!** What's a werewolf?" "Be quiet and go comb your face!"

"**Mommy, Mommy!** What's for dinner?" "Shut up and get back in the oven!"

"**Mommy, Mommy!** When will the paddling pool be full?" "Shut up and keep spitting!"

"**Mommy, Mommy!** Why are we pushing the car off the cliff?" "Shut up or you'll wake your father!"

"**Mommy, Mommy!** Why are you moaning?" "Shut up and keep licking!"

"**Mommy, Mommy!** Why do I have to hop everywhere?" "Shut up, or I'll chop off the other leg!"

"**Mommy, Mommy!** Why is Daddy bent over and crying?" "Just shut up and eat your hot dog!"

"**Mommy, Mommy!** Why is Daddy running away?" "Shut up and reload!"

Movie Theaters

A man in a movie theater sees a young woman sitting by herself. He notices that she has both hands up her skirt and is fingering herself furiously. He moves next to her and offers to help. The woman is glad to accept, so the man starts fingering her like crazy. Eventually he gets tired and has a rest. As soon as he takes his hand away, the woman dives in again and starts fingering once more. "What's the matter?" asks the man. "Wasn't I good enough?" "You were great," the woman replies. "But these crabs just won't stop!"

• • • • •

Billy gets to play his guitar on a movie soundtrack. He's very proud of his work but finds out that the movie is a porno film. Normally Billy wouldn't be seen dead watching hard-core movies, but he wants to hear his music so he sneaks into the local porno theater. Billy takes a seat near a little old lady and watches as the film starts. He is horrified by the non-stop orgy on the screen and, just when he can't imagine things getting any more depraved, a large German Shepherd joins in the action. The dog proceeds to have sex with all the women and most of the men. When the film finally ends, the lights go up and Billy puts on his coat. He catches the eye of the old lady and says, "I don't normally watch this sort of thing—I only wanted to hear my music on the soundtrack." "That's alright," replies the little old lady. "I only came here to see my dog!"

Names

Bob starts talking to a girl in a bar and asks her name. "I call myself 'Carmen,'" she replies. "It's not my real name, but it reflects my two main interests in life: fast cars and sexy men. So, what's your name, handsome?" Bob thinks for a moment, then says, "Beerfuck!"

•••••

Three women, with boyfriends all named "Billy," are talking in a bar. One says, "I'm tired of getting my Billy mixed up with your Billys. Why don't we all name our Billy after a soda pop? I'll name my Billy '7-Up' because he has seven inches and it's always up!" The second woman says, "I'll name my Billy 'Mountain Dew' because my Billy can 'mount' and 'dew' me anytime!" The third woman says, "I'm gonna name my Billy 'Jack Daniels.'" "Jack Daniels?" says the first woman. "That's not a soda, that's a hard liquor!" The third woman replies, "Yup, that's my Billy!"

Newlyweds

A man returns from his honeymoon and his friend asks him how it went. "Terrible," he replies. "On the first night I got up to go to the bathroom and, without thinking, I put a

$50 bill on her pillow." "Well, that's not so bad," replies the friend. "If she's upset, tell her it was a joke." "She wasn't upset," replies the man. "I got upset when she gave me $30 change!"

•••••

A newly married couple are in their hotel honeymoon suite when the wife bangs her foot on the bathroom door. "Oh, dear, honey-bun!" croons her husband. "Come here and I'll kiss your tootsie-wootsies better for you." She goes over to him and he kisses her toe better. Things develop and soon they're making love. Afterward the woman gets up to go to the bathroom and, again, bangs her foot on the door. Her husband calls out, "Will you watch where you're going, you clumsy bitch!"

•••••

A newly married husband lays down some rules. "I'll be home when I want, if I want, and at what time I want," he insists. "And, I don't expect any hassle from you. Also, I expect a decent meal to be on the table every evening, unless I tell you otherwise. I'll go hunting, fishing, boozing and card playing with my buddies whenever I want. Those are my rules," he continues. "Any comments?" His new bride replies, "No, that's fine with me. But, just understand that there'll be sex here at seven o'clock every night... whether you're here or not!"

•••••

On their honeymoon a pair of newlyweds are arguing. The couple promised to be honest with each other, but the hus-band still won't tell his wife how many sex partners he's

had. "Look," he says. "If I tell you, you'll just get angry."
"No, I won't," she replies. "Cross my heart and hope to
die." "Okay," says the man. "Let me think. There was one,
two, three, four, five, you, seven, eight..."

•••••

A young couple have just gotten married and are about to
spend their first night together. The man says, "There's
something you ought to know—I'm hung like a baby." His
bride is disappointed but tells him that sex isn't the important thing: Love is what makes marriage special. Hearing
this, the husband takes off his pants and the woman faints.
When she's recovered, she says, "What the hell was that?
You said you were hung like a baby!" "I am," her husband
replies. "It's eight pounds and 20 inches!"

•••••

A young honeymoon couple rent a cottage from an old
lady. The cottage is in a beautiful countryside by a fishing
lake, but the couple spend all their time indoors. Finally,
the old lady knocks on the door to see if they're okay.
"We're fine," says the young man. "We're living on the
fruits of love." "I guessed as much," says the old lady. "But
would you mind not throwing the peelings out of the window—they're choking my ducks!"

•••••

On the day of her wedding a bride goes to her mother and
confesses that she's not a virgin. "How can I convince my
husband he's the first?" she asks. "It's easy," her mother
replies. "Put an elastic band round your thigh and when
he's goes into you, snap it against your leg. It will sound

like your hymen breaking." The bride puts this plan into action. That night, when her new husband mounts her, she snaps the band against her thigh. "What the hell was that?" cries her husband. "It must have been my hymen snapping," replies the wife. "Then snap it back again!" shouts the husband. "It's caught around my fucking nuts!"

•••••

On the night before her wedding an Italian bride-to-be asks her mother how she can make her husband happy. "Well, there's all sorts of things a wife can do with her husband in bed," her mother replies. "Mama," replies her daughter. "I know how to fuck! What I need is your meatball recipe!"

•••••

Ricardo gets married, but he's led a sheltered life and is unsure what to do on his wedding night. "For Christ's sake!" shouts his wife. "Take your clothes off and put that thing you play with in the place where I pee!" So Ricardo does as she asks. He gets undressed and puts his accordion in the toilet!

•••••

Three honeymooning couples settle down for the night in a hotel. One man sees his wife naked for the first time and cries, "My God! What a huge fat ass!" His furious bride throws him out into the corridor. The second man also sees his wife naked and cries, "Christ! What huge dangling tits!" He too is thrown into the corridor. A few moments later the third man is also thrown out. "Did you put your foot in it?" asks the first. "No," replies the third. "But I could have!"

•••••

Three sisters get married on the same day. They're a poor family and none of their husbands can afford a fancy honeymoon so the new couples stay over for a week at the girls' parents' house. On the first night of the triple honeymoon the mother walks past the guest rooms to go to the bathroom. From her eldest daughter's room she hears screaming; from her middle daughter's room she hears laughing, but from the youngest daughter's room she hears nothing at all. The next day she asks the eldest daughter why she was screaming so much. "Mama," she says, "You always told me that if I found something uncomfortable, I should make a noise about it." The mother then asks her middle daughter why she was laughing so much. "Mama," she replies, "You always said that if something tickled me, I shouldn't be afraid to laugh." Finally, the mother asks the youngest daughter why she'd been silent. "Mama," she replies, "You always taught me not to speak with my mouth full!"

•••••

Two grooms in a honeymoon hotel compare notes on their first night. "How did you leave your wife this morning?" asks one. "On the bed, smoking," the other replies. "Wow!" says the first. "Mine was just a bit sore!"

•••••

Why do honeymoons only last seven days? Because seven days make a whole week!

• • • • •

Why does a bride smile when she walks up the aisle? She knows she's given her last blow job!

Night Out

A man doing a survey stops three women in the street. "Ladies," he asks. "How do you know if you've had a good night out?" The first one says, "I've had a good night if I come home and I tingle all over." The second says, "I've had a good night if I come home and feel butterflies in my stomach." And the third says, "When I get home I rip off my underwear and chuck them at the window. If they stick to the glass, I know I've had a great night!"

• • • • •

A theatrical agent discovers that one of his clients, an attractive young actress, has taken up prostitution and asks to spend the night with her. The actress agrees but says that the agent must pay the full rate for the night. The agent pays up, so they go to bed, turn out the light and make love. Afterward the actress falls asleep but is woken up an hour later for more sex. After half an hour of passion the exhausted girl falls asleep, only to be woken again for yet more sex. This goes on and on, and, after six sessions, the actress can't take it any more. She switches on the light and finds a strange man in bed with her. "You're not my agent!" she cries, "No," the man replies. "He's at the door selling tickets!"

• • • • •

Bill's wife decides to take him to a lap-dancing club as a surprise birthday present. He protests but she drags him along anyway. At the entrance the manager greets him saying, "Hello, Bill. How are you doing?" "How does he know your name?" asks Bill's wife. "Er, I knew him from school," he explains. Inside the club the coatroom girl says, "Good evening, Bill. How are you tonight?" Bill hurriedly explains that she's a friend of a coworker. When they sit down the waitress comes up and says, "Great to see you, Bill. Would you like your usual?" Bill tells his wife that she's a member of his tennis club. Finally a pole dancer walks past and says, "Hi, Bill! Stay there and I'll come by and give you a special." This is too much for Bill's wife, who drags him outside and starts screaming at him. The doorman hails them a taxi. "Oh, boy, Bill," he says. "You sure picked an ugly one tonight!"

• • • • •

Three men walk into a strip bar. The first man licks a $100 bill and slaps it on one of the stripper's buttcheeks. The second man licks a $100 bill and slaps it on the stripper's other buttcheek. The third man takes out a credit card, swipes it through her butt crack and takes the $200.

Nudity

A couple take their young son to a nude beach. The boy notices that some of the ladies have breasts much bigger than his mother's, and asks her why. She explains, "The bigger they are, the dumber their owner." The boy goes to play in the water, but returns to tell his mother that many of the men have larger penises than his dad. His mother replies, "The bigger they are, the dumber their owner." Satisfied with this answer, the boy goes for a walk. Shortly after he returns. "Mommy," he says. "I just saw Daddy talking to the dumbest girl on the beach. And the longer they talked, the dumber he got!"

•••••

A man sunbathes in the nude and ends up burning his penis. His doctor tells him to ease the pain by dipping it in a saucer of cold milk. Later, his wife comes home and finds him with his dick in a saucer of milk. "Good heavens," she remarks. "I always wondered how you reloaded those things!"

•••••

Did you hear about the flasher who was thinking of retiring? He decided to stick it out for one more year!

•••••

Three old women were sitting on a park bench when a man jumped out and flashed them. Two of the women had a stroke; the other couldn't reach.

•••••

We've introduced "dress down Friday" at our nudist colony. On Fridays none of us trim our bikini lines!

Numbers

What's a 6.9? A good thing screwed up by a period!
What's a 68? You do me and I'll owe you one!

Offspring

A couple and their ten-year-old son live in an apartment in the city. They decide that the only way they can have a Sunday afternoon quickie with their son in the apartment is to send him out on the balcony and get him to report on all the neighborhood activities. The couple go to bed and the boy begins his commentary, "There's a car being towed from the parking lot," he says. "An ambulance just drove by." A few moments pass. "Looks like the Andersons have company," he calls out. After a minute he says, "Hey, Matt's riding a new bike and the Coopers are having sex!" Shocked, his mom and dad sit up in bed. "How do you know the Coopers are having sex?" says Dad. The boy replies, "Because their kid is standing out on the balcony too!"

• • • • •

A couple have four sons. The oldest three are tall with red hair, while the youngest, Jason, is short and dark. After a long illness, the father is facing death. He turns to his wife and says, "Dearest, before I die, be honest—is Jason my son?" His wife replies, "Yes, he is, my darling. I swear it."

Hearing this the husband passes away peacefully. His wife lets out a sigh of relief, "Thank God he didn't ask about the other three!"

•••••

A woman has just given birth. The doctor comes over with her new baby boy after giving it a checkup. "Excuse me, miss," he says. "But your baby seems to be multicolored. I've never seen anything like it—his face has Chinese features." "Yeah," says the woman. "I heard those Chinese guys are pretty good, so I decided to give them a try." "Okay," says the doctor. "But his upper body is white." "Yeah," says the woman. "I heard them white fellers were pretty good, so I decided to give them a try." "But your baby has black legs," remarks the doctor. "Yeah," says the woman. "I heard them black men were pretty good, too, so I decided to give them a try as well." "Well, your baby's healthy, but he does looks a little odd," says the doctor. "Don't matter," the woman replies. "Let's just hope he don't start barking!"

•••••

A young man goes up to his father and says, "This is sort of embarrassing, but can I have twenty bucks for a blow job?" His father replies, "That depends... Are you any good?"

Old People

A horny young man is sitting on a park bench watching girls go by. "God, I sure would like to have a little pussy," he mutters to himself. A little old lady overhears him. "Me too, young man—mine's the size of a bucket!"

•••••

Eighty-year-old Willy marries 20-year-old Brittany. After a year Brittany goes into the hospital to give birth. The doctor congratulates the old man. "It's amazing," he says. "How do you do it at your age?" Willy answers, "You've just got to keep that old motor running, Doc." The following year Brittany gives birth again. The doctor comes up to Willy and remarks, "You're incredible—how do you manage it?" Again Willy answers, "You've just got to keep the old motor running, Doc." The next year Brittany goes back yet again. The doctor says, "Three kids at your age. You must be quite a man, Willy!" Willy responds with his usual phrase: "You've just got to keep that old motor running, Doc." The doctor looks embarrassed and says, "Well, you might be right, Willy. But I reckon it's time to change the oil—this baby's black!"

•••••

A 90-year-old man goes to his doctor for a physical. A few days later the doctor sees the old geezer walking down the street with a big, beautiful black lady on his arm. During the old man's next visit the doctor says, "I saw you in the street the other day. I notice you have a new lady friend." "Just doing what you told me, Doc," replies the old man. "'Get a hot mamma and be cheerful' is what you said." The doctor's face drops. "No," he replies. "I said, 'You've got a heart murmur—be careful'!"

•••••

A 90-year-old man marries a girl of 18. On their wedding night he slips into bed and holds up four fingers. "Wow!" says his bride. "Does that mean we're going to have sex four times?" "No," he replies. "It means take your pick!"

•••••

A senile old lady is in a nursing home. She's in a wheelchair and every day she wheels herself up and down the corridors making "car" sounds. One day an old man jumps out of a doorway and says, "Excuse me, ma'am, but you were speeding. Can I see your driver's license?" The old lady digs around in her purse and pulls out a candy wrapper. The old man looks at it and tells her she can go. A little while later the old man jumps out of a doorway and says, "Excuse me, ma'am, but I saw you cross the center line back there. Can I see your registration please?" The old lady hands him a scrap of newspaper. He takes a look and then sends her on her way. A little while later the old lady is zooming along when she hits a fire extinguisher. The old man jumps out of a doorway and opens his dressing gown to reveal a huge erection. "Oh, dang it!" says the old lady. "Not the breathalyzer again!"

•••••

What did one saggy boob say to the other? If we don't get some support soon, people are going to think we're nuts!

•••••

What does a 75-year-old woman have between her breasts that a 25-year-old doesn't? Her navel!

• • • • •

A 60-year-old man joins an exclusive nudist swingers' club. After stripping naked he wanders around, sees a gorgeous woman and gets an erection. The woman notices this, comes over and asks, "Did you call for me?" The man replies, "No—what do you mean?" "You must be new here," replies the woman. "Let me explain. It's a rule that if you get an erection, it implies you called for me." She then leads the man into a chalet, where they have incredible sex. Later, the man continues to look around and goes into the sauna. As he sits down, he farts. A huge, fat hairy man lumbers out of the steam towards him. "Did you call for me?" he asks. "I don't think so," replies the newcomer. "You must be new here," says the hairy man. "It's a rule that if you fart, it implies you called for me." The huge hairy man then bends the newcomer over a bench and has his way with him. Later, the man hobbles back to the club's office and finds the receptionist. "I want to cancel my membership," he says. "But, sir," she replies. "You've only been here for a few hours—you haven't had a chance to see all our facilities." "Yeah, well I'm not interested," says the man. "I'm 60 years old, I get a hard-on once a month and I fart about fifteen times a day!"

• • • • •

A teenage girl comes downstairs to meet her date. The girl's grandma is horrified to see that she's wearing a see-through top and no bra. "You can't go out looking like that!" she says. "Oh, be quiet!" snaps the girl. "This is the 21st century—I can let my rosebuds show if I want to!"

With that she storms out of the house. The next evening the girl hears her boyfriend ring the doorbell and comes downstairs to go on another date. She walks into the hallway and finds that grandma has answered the door and is chatting to the young man. However, she's astonished to see that grandma is topless and her huge wrinkled boobs are swinging down past her navel. "Grandma!" shouts the girl. "What the hell are you doing?" "Oh, you be quiet!" snaps grandma. "If you can show off your rosebuds, I can sure as hell display my hanging baskets!"

•••••

Why is getting a blow job from an 80-year-old like walking a tightrope? In both cases you don't really want to look down!

•••••

An 85-year-old man marries a lovely 25-year-old woman. Because her new husband is so old, the woman decides they should have separate honeymoon suites to prevent the old man overexerting himself. On their wedding night there's a knock on the bride's door and the groom comes in, ready for action. After they've finished he leaves her and she prepares to get some sleep. A few minutes pass and there's another knock on the door. The bride opens it to find her husband ready for more action. They go back to bed, have sex and the old man leaves again. Once more the bride gets ready for sleep, but after a few minutes there's another knock and the elderly groom presents himself for another romp. Afterwards the young bride complements her husband on his stamina. "Three times in one night," she remarks.

"There aren't many men who could manage that." The old man looks confused and says, "Manage *what*?"

·····

An elderly woman returns home and finds her husband having sex with a young girl. Enraged, she flings him out of the window and watches him plummet to his death. At her trial she pleads not guilty to murder. "How can you plead not guilty?" asks the prosecuting lawyer. "You threw your husband to his death." "I didn't know he was going to die," the woman replies. "I reckoned if he could still screw around aged 98, there was a good chance the bastard could fly as well!"

·····

An elderly couple are standing at the bow of a cruise ship when a wave washes the old woman overboard. They search for days, but can't find her and eventually the old man goes home. After three weeks he gets a telegram from the Coast Guard saying "Sorry to inform you that your wife is dead. Her body has been dredged up from the seafloor by a fishing boat. On examination an oyster was found inside her privates. Inside the oyster was a pearl worth $50,000. Please advise." The old man telegraphs back, "Send me the pearl and re-bait the trap."

·····

An old couple are sitting on their sofa when the woman suddenly punches her husband, knocking him off his seat. "What did you do that for?" asks the old man. His wife replies, "I hit you because your dick is way too small!" The old man sits down and then punches his wife, knocking her to the floor. "Why did you do that?" she asks. He replies, "For knowing the difference after sixty years of marriage!"

•••••

An old couple get married after many years of courtship. On their honeymoon night the husband takes off his glasses and goes to clean his teeth. In the meantime his bride decides to limber up. She strips naked and does a stretching exercise, lying on her back and lifting her legs up and over her head. Unfortunately, her feet get stuck in the headboard and she cries out for help. Her husband dashes in, peers at her and says, "For God's sake, Muriel! Brush your hair and put in your teeth… You look just like your mother!"

•••••

An old man goes to the doctor for an annual checkup. He's a bit deaf so he brings his wife along to help out. The doctor says, "To do the correct tests I'll need to see a urine sample, a feces sample and a sperm sample." The man cups his hand to his ear and cries, "What… what did you say?" His wife shouts, "The doctor says he wants to see your underwear!"

•••••

An old man walks shakily through the door of a Nevada brothel and is accosted by the doorman. "You gotta be in the wrong place," says the doorman. "What the hell you looking for, old timer?" The old man replies, "Is this where all the gals are ready for hire? Cos I'm a hankering for a good time." "Just how old are you, Pops?" asks the doorman. "92," the old man replies. "92!" exclaims the doorman. "Boy, you've had it, Grandpa." A moment of confusion crosses the old man's face, "Really?" he says, fumbling in his wallet. "How much do I owe you?"

•••••

An old man meets up with an old lady at a Bingo evening. They end up going back to her place, where they have sex. The man goes home but wakes the next morning to find his penis has developed a painful swelling and a persistent leaky discharge. Disturbed, he goes to his doctor. "Have you had sex recently?" asks the doctor. "Yes," the old man replies. "Do you know the woman's name?" he asks. "I do," says the old man. "And can you remember where she lives?" asks the doctor. "Certainly," replies the old man. "Then you'd better get back there as soon as you can," says the doctor. "You're about to come!"

•••••

Bill and Cheryl have become friendly in the retirement home. Things progress to the point where Bill goes to Cheryl's room every Friday night and gets jerked off. This goes on for a few months until Bill meets up with another little old lady and starts hanging around with her instead. "What's she got that I haven't got?" demands Cheryl. Bill replies, "Parkinson's!"

•••••

Doris and Bert are living in an old folks' home. They've been giving each other the eye for a while and finally decide to get together. They retire to Bert's room, where he asks Doris if there's anything she'd like to do. "Well, I do like a bit of cunnilingus," she says. Bert gets down to it, but he has to come up for air after a few seconds. "I'm sorry," says Bert. "I can't carry on—the smell down there is disgusting!" "Sorry," says Doris. "It must be my arthritis." "You can't have arthritis down there," replies Bert, "and if you could, it wouldn't smell." "No," explains Doris. "The arthritis is in my shoulders—it means I can't wipe my ass!"

• • • • •

How did the octogenarian car mechanic make love? He attached leads to his nipples and got a jumpstart from a younger man!

• • • • •

Old Hamish and his wife are watching an evangelist on the TV. The evangelist tells them to put one hand on the screen and touch any afflicted part of their body with the other. Hamish's wife totters over to the screen, touches the glass with one hand and places the other on her arthritic hip. Old Hamish decides to get in on the act. He totters over to the TV, places one hand on the screen and sticks the other up his kilt. "Hamish," says his wife. "Were ye no listening? The man's healing the sick, not raising the fucking dead!"

• • • • •

Here's the story of a woman who just turned 47: "When I was 16, I hoped one day I would have a boyfriend. When I was 18, I got a boyfriend, but there was no passion. In college I dated a passionate guy, but he was too emotional. When I was 25, I found a very stable guy, but he was too boring. When I was 28, I found an exciting guy, but he was directionless. When I was 31, I found a smart ambitious guy with his feet planted firmly on the ground and married him. After sixteen years he divorced me, took everything I owned and ran off with my best friend. I am now 47 and looking for a guy with a big dick!"

• • • • •

Two old men are discussing their sex lives. "You know what I do?" says one of the old men. "Every morning I eat half a loaf of rye bread—it's great for your dick; it lets you have really strong erections." The second old man decides to give this a go. He hobbles down to his local bakery and asks for a loaf of rye bread. "Sure," replies the clerk. "Do you want that whole or sliced?" "What's the difference?" asks the old man. "Well," the clerk replies. "If it's sliced, it'll go harder faster." "What?" whines the old man. "How come everyone knows about this except me?"

• • • • •

Two old men visit a whorehouse. The Madame takes one look at the pair and figures they're both so senile they won't be able to tell the difference between a real girl and a blow-up doll. She puts a doll in each of the old geezers' rooms, turns out the lights and lets them get on with it. After an hour of wheezing sex the old coots stagger out to a nearby bar. Over drinks they compare notes. The first man says, "Y'know, I think my gal was dead. She never moved a muscle, talked, or even groaned. How was it for you?" The second man replies, "I think mine was some kinda witch." "What d'you mean, witch?" asks the first. "Well, it's weird," says the second, "but when I bit her on the tit, she farted and flew out the window!"

•••••

Two old men, Joe and Manny, work on an assembly line in a factory. Joe keeps boasting about his sexual prowess and tells Manny that he made love to his wife three times on Sunday. "Three times!" gasps Manny. "How do you do it?" "It's easy," says Joe. "We had sex and then I rolled over and took a ten-minute nap. When I woke up, we made love again and I took another ten-minute nap. Then I put it to her again. The big secret is having rests in-between." "I gotta try that," says Manny. "Lorraine won't believe her luck." That night Manny makes love to his wife and then takes a nap. He wakes up, makes love again and takes another nap. He wakes up and makes love a third time and then falls sound asleep. When he next wakes up, he realizes he's overslept, so he pulls on his clothes and runs to the factory. Outside he finds his boss waiting for him, fuming. "What's up, boss?" asks Manny. "Why are you so cross? I've worked here for forty years and never been late. You aren't going to hold twenty minutes against me, are you?" "What do you mean 'twenty minutes'?" shouts the boss. "Where the hell were you on Monday and Tuesday?"

•••••

Why don't old ladies have Pap smears? Well, let's put it this way—have you ever tried to prie open a grilled cheese sandwich?

•••••

Two old men are walking through the park on a hot summer's day when they see a girl sunbathing in the nude. To hide her modesty the girl has a roofing tile placed between her legs. "Oh, hell," says one old man. "I can remember when they used to be thatched!"

One-Night Stands

After a huge drinking binge a man wakes one morning to find himself in a strange bed alongside the ugliest woman he's ever seen. Horrified, he slips out of bed and pulls on his clothes as quietly as possible. He's just about to sneak out when he feels a twinge of guilt, so he gets a $20 bill out of his pocket and puts it on a table. He feels a tug on his leg and looks down to see it's being pulled by another ugly girl, who's been asleep under a pile of clothes on the floor. "Hey!" she says. "Nothing for the bridesmaid?"

•••••

Larry meets a girl at a bar and they end up at her place. After a night of torrid sex he wakes up and starts to get dressed. As he's doing so, he notices a picture of a man on the dresser. The man looks very young and fit and Larry starts to worry that he might be a jealous boyfriend or husband. The girl is waking up, so Larry asks her, "Excuse me, but who's in the picture? It's not your husband, is it?" "Oh, no," the girl replies. "That was me before the operation!"

Orgasms

A farmer and his wife are lying in bed, reading. The farmer looks up from his magazine and says, "This feller writes here that humans are the only species in which the female achieves orgasm?" His wife replies, "Well, how on earth would anyone find that out?" "You're right," says the farmer thoughtfully. "How would they know?" "Dang it!" he says and gets out of bed, puts on a bathrobe and walks out the door. An hour later he comes back red in the face. "Well, that was a waste of time," he says. "I'm pretty sure the cow and sheep didn't, but the way that pig is always squealing, how can you tell?"

• • • • •

An old man marries a much younger lady. However, no matter what he tries, he can never give his wife an orgasm. He goes to a sex therapist and tells him the problem. "What you've got to do is encourage your wife to fantasize," says the therapist. "Hire a young man to stand at your bedside and get him to wave a towel while you have sex." Though puzzled, the old man agrees to give it a go. He hires a young bodybuilder to stand over the couple the next time they have sex. The bodybuilder stands by waving a towel but still the wife won't orgasm. The old man goes back to the therapist, who suggests the old man and the bodybuilder swap positions. That night the bodybuilder and the wife have sex while the old man stands at the bedside waving a towel. In a very short time the wife has a series of earth-shattering orgasms. "Hah!" shouts the old man, slapping the bodybuilder's butt. "Now THAT'S the way to wave a fucking towel!"

• • • • •

How can a woman tell if she's having a really great orgasm? Her husband wakes up!

•••••

How do you tell when a blonde reaches orgasm? The next person in the line taps you on the shoulder.

•••••

My wife and I achieved simultaneous orgasm last night. Unfortunately she was in bed with my brother and I was watching from inside a closet!

•••••

Why do women have multiple orgasms? So they can fucking moan when they're happy, too!

Parasites

A flea is sitting on a dog when a second flea hops by, complaining about the weather. "Damn, it's cold!" he says. "I've been living in a biker's moustache for the last month—it's freezing out on the road." The first flea replies, "I know a good way to get warm. Go to the airport and wait in the ladies' bathroom. When you see a flight attendant, climb into her pubes and you'll be flown somewhere warm and sunny." The second flea agrees to give this a go, but a week later he's back, complaining about the cold again. "Hey," says the first flea. "Didn't you go to the airport?" "Yeah," says the second flea. "And I climbed into a flight attendant's pubes like you said, but half an hour later I was back in that damn biker's moustache again!"

• • • • •

An old miser goes looking for the cheapest whore he can find. He eventually finds one standing by a dumpster who'll do it for $10. He takes her to the cheapest motel he can find and they get down to business. A few weeks later he sees the prostitute standing by the dumpster again. "Hey, you!" he shouts. "You dirty bitch! You gave me crabs!" The woman shouts back, "What did you expect for $10… lobster?"

Parrots

A woman goes into a pet shop to buy a parrot. She's shown a beautiful bird for $20. "Why is it so cheap?" she asks. "It used to live in a brothel," explains the salesclerk, "and now its language is a bit fruity." "Oh, I don't mind that," says the woman. "I'm very broad-minded." She takes the parrot home, where it looks around and says, "Fuck me, a new brothel and a new madam." "I'm not a madam and this isn't a brothel," replies the woman indignantly. A little later the woman's two teenage daughters arrive home. "Well, fuck me—a new brothel, a new madam and now new whores!" cries the parrot. "These are my daughters, not prostitutes," says the woman indignantly. A short while later the woman's husband comes home. "Well, fuck me!" says the parrot. "A new brothel, a new madam, new whores, but the same old clients… How ya doing, Dave?"

• • • • •

An old man and a parrot have lived together for over forty years. One day the parrot says, "You know, I've never had sex in my life—I'd really like to try it before I die." The old man agrees to help and takes the parrot to a nearby pet shop, where there are lots of female parrots, but they're all too expensive—$40 is the most the old man can raise and the cheapest parrot is $250. The shop owner takes pity on the old man and his horny parrot and says they can rent a female for the night for forty bucks. The old man and the parrot go home with the female, and the old man puts the two birds in a room to get on with it. After a minute the man hears a terrible squawking. He runs into the room, where he finds his parrot tearing the feathers off the female. "What are you doing?" shouts the old man. "What does it look like?" replies the parrot. "For forty bucks, I should at least get to see this chick naked!"

Party Time

A man has a costume party where the guests have to come as a human emotion. On the big night the first guest arrives covered in green paint with the letters "N" and "V" painted on his chest. "Great outfit," says the host. "What emotion is that?" The guest replies, "I'm green with en-vy." A few minutes later, the host opens the door to a woman covered in a pink body stocking with a feather boa wrapped around her intimate parts. "And what emotion are you?" asks the host. The guest replies, "I'm tickled pink." Next, the host opens the door to two of his Jamaican friends, Winston and Leroy. Winston is stark naked with his penis stuck in a bowl of custard and Leroy is stark naked with his penis stuck in a pear. "And what sort of emotions are those?" asks the host.

Winston replies, "Well, I'm fucking disgusted, and Leroy has come in despair!"

• • • • •

A man takes early retirement and leaves the big city for a cottage in the Scottish Highlands. After a month of isolation he hears a knock on his door. He answers it and finds an enormous Scottish farmer standing outside. "I hear you're new around here," says the farmer, "Yes, I am," the man replies. "I thought I'd introduce myself," says the farmer, "and invite you to a party I'm having." "That's very nice—I'd love to come," says the man. "I'd better warn you, there'll be lots of drinking," the farmer continues. "I don't mind—I like to drink," the man replies. "And nee doubt there'll be a few fights breaking oot," says the farmer. "That's okay, I can take care of myself," replies the man. "And things get a bit frisky in the wee hours," says the farmer. "There'll be lots o' sex." "That's fine by me," says the man. "I haven't had any female company for a long time." "Oh, there'll be no lassies," says the farmer. "It's just the two of us!"

• • • • •

A man turns up at a costume party wearing only a pair of pants. "And what are you?" asks the host. "A premature ejaculation," the man replies. "I just came in my pants!"

• • • • •

I went to a costume party last night, where I saw a woman completely naked except for a pair of black gloves and a pair of black boots. She'd come as the five of spades!

• • • • •

Julian goes up to Billy and asks, "Here, if you went to a wild party, got drunk and woke up with a condom sticking out of your ass, would you tell anyone?" "No," replies Billy. "I see," says Julian. "In that case, do you want to come to a party?"

Penguins

A man walks into a seedy brothel. "What can I get for $5?" he asks. "Not much," the madam replies. "But I suppose you might get a penguin." The man isn't sure what a "penguin" is but, being desperate, he hands over his cash. The madam takes him to a back room and tells him to drop his pants. A prostitute then comes in and starts to give him a fantastic blow job. He's just about to come when the prostitute gets up and leaves. The man waddles after her with his pants around his ankles. "Hey!" he shouts. "What the fuck is a penguin?"

Penises

What's the worst part of a man's body? His penis—it has a head with no brains, hangs out with two nuts and lives around the corner from an asshole!

• • • • •

A man marries a girl from a very sheltered background. On their first night together he shows her his penis and, thinking it might stop her playing around in the future, tells her it's the only one in the world. A week later his bride says, "You remember that thing you showed me? You said you had the only one in the world." "That's right," replies the man. "Well, it's not true," says the bride. "The man next door has one, too." The man replies, "Well, yes… I used to have two of them, but that man is a good friend, so I gave him one of mine." His wife whines, "Awww, but why did you have to give him the *best* one?"

• • • • •

A little boy and girl are talking. "What's a penis?" asks the little girl. "I'm not sure," the boy replies. "I'll ask my dad." The boy goes off and finds his father lying on the couch. "What's a penis?" asks the boy. The dad unzips his fly and shows him. "This is a penis—as a matter of fact it's the perfect penis!" The boy takes a look and then runs off to find his friend. He unzips his fly and shows the little girl what's inside. "This is a penis," says the boy. "And if it was two inches shorter, it would be the perfect penis!"

• • • • •

A Texan walks into a bar and says, "Last week my wife gave birth to a 20-pound baby boy and I'd like to buy everyone a drink!" He buys a round of drinks and the bartender remarks, "20 pounds is a pretty big baby. What does he weigh now?" "15 pounds," replies the Texan. "How could he lose so much weight in a week?" asks the bartender. "That's easy," the Texan replies. "We had him circumcised!"

• • • • •

Did you hear about the man who had a penis transplant? His hand rejected it!

•••••

What do you call the useless piece of skin on the end of a penis? A man!

•••••

Little Johnny is in school sitting through a sex education video. At the end he says to teacher, "That video was wrong! Some guys have two dicks, not just one." "No, Johnny," says the teacher. "All men just have the one." "But my dad's got two," says Little Johnny. "A little one for going to the bathroom and a big one to clean mom's teeth!"

Penises: Well-Endowed

A big Texan ambles into the men's room of a Dallas hotel. He stands at the urinal and notices that the little guy standing next to him has an enormous dick. "Jesus! How long is that?" asks the Texan. "Fourteen inches," replies the little guy, proudly. "Hoowee!" exclaims the Texan. "Fourteen inches soft?" "That's right," says the little man. "So how long is it hard?" asks the Texan. The little guy shrugs; "Dunno—every time it gets stiff, I pass out!"

•••••

A man is shipwrecked on a desert island and survives alone for thirty years. One day a beautiful woman is washed ashore. She asks him how he's managed to survive so long on a barren island. "I pick berries and dig for clams," replies the man. "And what do you do for sex?" asks the woman. "Sex?" cries the man. "It's been so long that I've forgotten how to do it!" "Then let me show you," responds the woman, which she then does—three times in a row. "So what did you think of it?" asks the woman once they've finished. "That was great," replies the man. "But look what you did to my clam-digger!"

•••••

A man races into the men's restroom. He runs up to the urinal and whips out his twelve-inch dick. "Phew," he cries. "I just made it!" The man next to him looks over and says, "I like it—can you make me one, too?"

•••••

A white guy is talking to his well-hung black friend. "Say," asks the white guy. "Have you got any tips on increasing penis size? I'd like one as big as your monster!" "Well," the black guy replies, "I did hear this one trick: What you do is tie an elastic band around the base of your dick, then whack it with a mallet every morning and every evening for a month. They say it'll make a dick swell up to three times its normal size." The white guy agrees to give it a go and a month later he comes by to show his friend the result. "Mmm!" says the black guy, looking at his friend's dick. "It ain't nearly as big as mine." "No," his friend replies. "But at least it's turning the same color!"

•••••

A woman is divorcing her husband on the grounds of cruelty: His organ is so large it hurts her to have sex. After explaining her problem to a lawyer he tells her that he'll file her petition. "Screw that!" says the woman. "Why can't you go around and sandpaper his down a bit?"

• • • • •

A young man is so well-endowed it's interfering with his walking. Three doctors are consulted to solve the problem and they all recommend reductive surgery. The first doctor says, "We'll take a piece off the end." However, it's decided that this will affect his sensitivity. The second doctor says, "We'll just take a section out of the middle." This is discussed, but it's decided it will reduce the strength of the organ. The third doctor says, "Why not take a section out of the base?" This is also discussed, but they decide it will result in erection problems. Finally, a group of nurses present a petition saying, "Can't we just make his legs longer?"

• • • • •

A young man walks into a drugstore owned by a couple of spinsters. "This is very embarrassing," says the man. "But I have a problem with my penis—it's ten inches long and it never gets soft, even after making love for hours at a time. What can you give me for it?" The spinsters go to the back of the shop and have a muttered conversation. Eventually, one of them returns to the counter and says, "The best we can offer you is $500 a week and a third interest in the store!"

• • • • •

Bruce, to Mary: "I've got a ten-inch penis." Mary: "I find that hard to swallow!"

• • • • •

Did you hear about the guy who had three cocks? He used to love fucking women left, right and center!

• • • • •

Mr. Jones goes to his doctor and tells him that when he's in bed with his wife he can't get an erection. "Bring her back with you tomorrow," says the doctor. "We'll see what I can do." The next day Mr. Jones returns with his wife. "Take off your clothes, Mrs. Jones," says the doctor. "Now turn around and lie down please. Uh-huh, I see... Okay, you may put your clothes back on." The doctor takes Mr. Jones aside. "You're in perfect health," he says. "Your wife didn't give me an erection, either!"

• • • • •

Three men—an American, an Australian and a German— are bragging about how long their penises are. To put them to the test, they go to the top of a ten-story building and take turns flopping their penises over the side. The German goes first and his penis dangles down five stories. The next, it's the Australian and his dangles down eight stories. The American goes last, flops his over the side, then starts frantically twitching his hips about. "What are you doing, mate?" asks the Australian. The American replies, "Dodging traffic!"

• • • • •

Two brothers enlist in the Army. During their physical the doctor is surprised to find that both brothers have incredibly long penises. "How do you account for this?" he asks. "It's hereditary, sir," explains the older brother. "I see," says the doctor, "Your father is the reason for your elongated penises." "No, sir—our mother is," the younger brother replies. "How could that be?" asks the doctor. "Women don't have penises!" "I know, sir," says the older brother.

"But she only had the one arm and when it came to getting us out of the bath, she had to manage as best she could!"

Penises: Not So Well-Endowed

A man goes to a doctor and asks him to look at his penis. "But you must promise not to laugh," says the man. The doctor agrees but when the man drops his pants, he can't help but snigger. "I'm sorry," he says. "But that's the tiniest penis I ever saw—it's so incredibly small, I can barely see it. So, anyway what seems to be the trouble with it?" The man replies, "It's swollen!"

• • • • •

A bodybuilder picks up a woman at a bar and takes her home. He takes off his shirt and the woman exclaims, "What a great chest you have!" The man replies, "That's 1000 pounds of dynamite!" He takes off his pants and the woman remarks, "What massive calves you have!" The bodybuilder replies, "That's 500 pounds of dynamite!" He then takes off his underwear. The woman takes one look and runs out of the apartment, screaming. He chases after her and asks why she ran. The woman replies, "I was afraid to be around all that dynamite when I saw what a short fuse you have!"

• • • • •

A man makes an obscene phone call to a woman. "Hello, darling," he gasps. "If you can guess what's in my hand, I'll give you a piece of the action." "Forget it," says the woman. "If you can hold it in one hand, I'm not interested!"

• • • • •

A man says to his wife, "You know what—two inches more, and I'd be King." She replies, "Two inches less, and you'd be Queen!"

Penises: My Dick Is So Big That...

My dick is so big, a homeless family lives underneath it.

My dick is so big, black holes fall into it.

My dick is so big, movie theaters now serve popcorn in small, medium, large and "my dick" sizes.

My dick is so big, compasses don't function properly near it.

My dick is so big, erections cause a total eclipse.

My dick is so big, FedEx won't insure it.

My dick is so big, I can change channels without the remote.

My dick is so big, I decorate it at Christmas time.

My dick is so big, I entered a Big Dick Contest and it came in first, second and third.

My dick is so big, I have to call it "Mister Dick" in company.

My dick is so big, I have to cook it breakfast.

My dick is so big, I lost my legs in Vietnam and can still drive a car with a manual transmission.

My dick is so big, I rent it out for weddings and Bar-Mitzvahs.

My dick is so big, I run three-legged races by myself.

My dick is so big, if I didn't sleep on my side, planes would crash into it at night.

My dick is so big, if I were a porn star, I could only make movies in wide-screen.

My dick is so big, I'm already fucking a girl tomorrow.

My dick is so big, I'm listed as an organ donor twice on my driver's license.

My dick is so big, it can chew gum.

My dick is so big, it could feed Ethiopia for a month.

My dick is so big, it gives me an allowance.

My dick is so big, it graduated a year before I did.

My dick is so big, it has a basement.

My dick is so big, it has a horizon.

My dick is so big, it has a moon.

My dick is so big, it has a personal trainer.

My dick is so big, it has a star on the Hollywood Walk of Fame.

My dick is so big, it has a stunt double.

My dick is so big, it has an entourage.

My dick is so big, it has an opening act.

My dick is so big, it has bark.

My dick is so big, it has branches.

My dick is so big, it has its own dick.

My dick is so big, it has its own zip code.

My dick is so big, it has reinforced foundations.

My dick is so big, it has tonsils.

My dick is so big, it has training wheels.

My dick is so big, it killed its ex-wife and got away with it.

My dick is so big, it made the Grand Canyon scream "Nooooooo!!"

My dick is so big, it snubbed the Oscars.

My dick is so big, it was recently split into two area codes.

My dick is so big, it won't return Spielberg's calls.

My dick is so big, it's going to be the opening act on the next Rolling Stones tour.

My dick is so big, it's in a boy band with four other dicks.

My dick is so big, it's in the Harlem Globetrotters.

My dick is so big, King Kong is going to climb up it in the next remake.

My dick is so big, Michael Jackson wants to build an amusement park on it.

My dick is so big, my mother was in labor for three extra days.

My dick is so big, my urologist is a Sherpa.

My dick is so big, one side never sees the sun.

My dick is so big, premature ejaculation takes ninety minutes.

My dick is so big, right now it's in the other room fixing us drinks.

My dick is so big, sperm banks pay me interest.

My dick is so big, Stephen Hawking has a theory about it.

My dick is so big, that I look like its dick in front of it.

My dick is so big that when I fly, it has to take the train.

My dick is so big, the doctor had to use a chainsaw to circumcise me.

My dick is so big, they're making a movie called *Godzilla versus My Dick*.

My dick is so big, there's still snow on it in summertime.

My dick is so big, when it gets hard Earth develops an elliptical orbit.

My dick is so big, you must be at least 48 inches to ride.

My dick is so big, its head has only seen my balls in pictures.

Penises: Euphemisms for the Penis

Admiral Winky.

The Albino Cave Dweller.

The Ambassador.

The Ankle Spanker.

The Bacon Bazooka.

The Bald Avenger.

The Baloney Pony.

The Bearded Burglar.

Beastus Maximus.

The Beaver Cleaver.

The Bed Snake.

The Beef Baton.

The Beef Thermometer.

Big Dick and the Twins.

The Bow-Legged Swamp Donkey.

The Caped Crusader.

The Cattle Prod.

The Cervical Crusader.

Charlie Russell, the One-Eyed Muscle.

The Chimney Cleaner.

The Chubby Conquistador.

Circus Goy.

The Clam Digger.

The Colon Cowboy.

Curious George.

The Custard Cannon.

Darth Vader.

The Deep-Veined Purple-Helmeted Spartan of Love.

Dora, the Anal Explorer.

Dr. Cyclops.

The Early Riser.

Earthworm Jim.

El Presidente.

Elmer, the Glue Shooter.

The Everlasting Gob-Dropper.

Excalibur.

The Fallopian Fiddler.

The Fandangled Mandangler.

Fat Albert.

The Fleshy Winnebago.

The Foaming Beef Probe.

Hairy Scary and the Two Bald Men.

The Hammer of Thor.

Handy Andy.

The Heat-Seeking Moisture Missile.

Homo Erectus.

The Hooded Warrior.

The Incredible Bulk.

Ivan the Terrible.

The Juicy Dangler.

The Lance of Love.

Lewinsky's Lunch.

The Love Lollipop.

The Love Torpedo.

The Love Truncheon.

The Lung Puncturer.

The Man in the Purple Helmet.

The Melon Baster.

The Midnight Wangler.

Mighty Joe Young.

Mr. Johnson and the Juice Crew.

Mr. Wobbly.

The Muff Marauder.

The One-Eyed Trouser Snake.

The One-Eyed Trouser Trout.

The One-Eyed Wonder Weasel.

The One-String Banjo.

The Perpendicular bisector.

The Pleasure Missile.

The Pocket Rocket.

The Pork Sword.

The Porridge Pump.

The Presidential Podium.

The Pump-Action Yogurt Rifle.

The Purple avenger.

The Purple Pulsating Pillar of Power.

The Pajama Python.

Ralph, the Fur-Faced Chicken.

The Reaming Tower of Penis.

The Rod of Power.

The Schlongmaster 2000.

The Sheep Shifter.

The Spam Javelin.

The Sperminator.

The Tennessee Throat-Warmer.

The Thadge Navigator.

The Three-Inch Punisher.

The Thrill-Drill.

Thunderbird Six.
Tiny Elvis.
The Tummy Banana.
The Turd Burglar.
The Twelve-Inch Train of Pain.
Uncle Wiggly.
The Vagina Miner.
The Vaginal Depth Detector.
Veinous Maximus.
Vlad the Impaler.
Wally, the One-Eyed Wonder Wiener.
The Weapon of Ass Destruction.
The Wibbly-Wobbly Semen Sausage.
The Womb Broom.
The Zipper Ripper.

Perfume

A woman walks up to a perfume counter and picks up a sample bottle. She sprays scent on her wrist and smells it. "That's nice," she says to the salesclerk, "What's it called?" The clerk replies, "It's 'Viens à moi.' That's French for 'Come to me.'" The woman takes another sniff and says, "Are you sure? It doesn't smell like come to me!"

Pets

A woman takes her two dachshunds, a male and a female, to the vet for a checkup. "Has the male been neutered?"

asks the vet. "There's no need," the woman replies. "At home I keep the female upstairs and the male downstairs. There's no chance they'll have puppies." "Can't the male climb stairs?" asks the vet. "No," the woman replies. "Not when he's got a hard-on!"

•••••

How do you make a dog drink? Put it in a blender!

•••••

How do you know when your cat's finished cleaning himself? He's smoking a cigarette.

•••••

Why don't bunnies make a noise when they make love? Because they have cotton balls.

•••••

A cute little girl walks into a pet shop and asks whether they have any bunny rabbits. "Well, sure," says the shopkeeper. "We have pretty bunnies with long floppy ears, and funny bunnies that hop around all day, or we even have fuzzy bunnies with thick fur that's fun to stroke. Which sort would you like?" The little girl replies, "I dunno—to be honest, I don't think Dad's python gives a shit!"

•••••

A little girl is out with her grandmother when they come across a couple of dogs mating. "What are they doing, Grandma?" asks the little girl. Her grandmother explains, "Well, the dog on top has hurt his paw, so the one underneath is carrying him to the doctor." "They're just like people, aren't they Grandma?" remarks the girl. "How do you mean?" asks her grandmother. The little girl replies, "Offer someone a helping hand and they fuck you every time!"

• • • • •

A man is having a drink in a country bar when he's approached by an old peasant carrying a sack. "You see this sack?" says the peasant. "In here, I got a ferret and this ferret will give you the best blow job you've ever had. If you want, you can buy him for $50." The man is not impressed and tells the peasant to go away. The peasant persists. "If you don't believe me," he says, "why not take it round the back and try it out." The man decides he might as well and goes around the back of the bar with the peasant. The ferret is brought out of the sack and proceeds to give the man an incredible blow job. After he's finished the man hands the peasant $50 and runs home with the animal. The man finds his wife in the kitchen and hands her the creature. "See that ferret?" he says. "That ferret just gave me the best oral sex I ever had." "Oh, yes," says the wife. "And what do you want me to do with it?" The man replies, "I want you to teach it to cook, then fuck off!"

• • • • •

What did the gerbil say when the gay guy walked into the pet store? "Woof! Woof-woof-woof…!"

• • • • •

What did the vet say to the dog who kept licking his balls? "Good boy!"

• • • • •

What do you call an adolescent rabbit? A pubic hare.

Photography

Wilbur has been summoned to his attorney's office. "Do you want the bad news first, or the terrible news first?" asks his lawyer. "Give me the bad news," says Wilbur. "Your wife just found a picture worth a million dollars," says the lawyer. "That's *bad* news?" asks Wilbur. "Well then, I can't wait to hear the terrible news." The lawyer replies, "The picture is of you having sex with a goat and a choir boy!"

Pick-Up Lines

Do you have any Irish in you? Would you like some?

Do you sleep on your stomach? Can I?

Do you want to fuck, or should I apologize?

Do you want to see something swell?

Do you work for the Postal Service? I could have sworn I saw you checking out my package.

Hey, baby! Why don't you sit on my lap and we'll talk about the first thing that pops up?

Hey, baby! Can I tickle your belly button from the inside?

Hey, baby! Let's play Army—I'll lay down and you can blow me up.

Hi, I've been undressing you with my eyes all night long—it's time to see if I'm right.

How about you sit on my lap and we'll straighten something out?

I lost my puppy. Can you help me find him? I think he went into a cheap motel room.

I may not be Fred Flintstone, but I sure can make your bed rock!

I want to kiss you passionately on the lips, and then move up to your belly button.

I was about to go and masturbate and I needed a name to go with your face.

I'd like to wrap your legs around my head and wear you like a feedbag.

If it's true that we are what we eat, then I could be you by morning.

If you were a car door, I'd slam you all night long.

If your left leg is Thanksgiving, and your right leg is Christmas, can I visit you in-between the holidays?

Is that a keg in your pants? 'Cause I'd just love to tap that ass!

I've got the hot dog and you've got the buns.

I've just received government funding for a four-hour expedition to find your G-spot.

Let's go back to my place and do the things I'm going to tell people we did anyway.

Man: "My magic watch tells me you aren't wearing underwear." Woman: "Well, your 'magic watch' is wrong." Man: "Oh, I'm sorry. It must be an hour fast."

Miss, if you've lost your virginity, can I have the package it came in?

My face is leaving in fifteen minutes—be on it!

My love for you is like diarrhea—I just can't hold it in!

Nice legs… What time do they open?

Roses are red, violets are blue… I like spaghetti—let's go fuck!

Screw me if I'm wrong, but is your name Helga?

Sit on my face and I'll guess your weight.

Somebody farted! Let's get out of here!

That outfit would look great in a crumpled heap on my bedroom floor tomorrow morning.

The word of the day is "legs." Let's go back to my place and spread the word.

What do you say we go back to my room and do some math? Add a bed, subtract our clothes, divide your legs and multiply!

Sit on my face and let me eat my way to your heart.

You know, if I were you, I'd have sex with me.

You with those curves, and me with no brakes...

You. Me. Whipped cream. Handcuffs. Any questions?

You're like a championship bass—I don't know if I should mount you, or eat you.

You've got 206 bones in your body. Would you like one more?

Politics

A Republican man is going out with a Democratic woman. One night they have an argument and the woman gives a frosty response when her boyfriend asks, "Is there any chance of the Republican being admitted to Congress tonight?" "No," she tells him. "The Democratic Party is firmly united at the present time and they will not be letting in any Republicans tonight." A little while later her mood changes and she says, "The Democratic Party has now been split wide open. If the Republican member stands now, there's a very good chance he'll get in." "I'm sorry," says her boyfriend. "The Republican has just stood as an Independent—and he's lost his deposit!"

•••••

A little old lady in Florida calls the police. "Help!" she cries. "Send a car to my house right away! There's a damn Democrat masturbating on my front porch!" "How d'you know the masturbator is a Democrat?" asks the operator. The little old lady replies, "It's obvious—if he was a Republican, he'd be screwing somebody!"

Premature Ejaculation

Patient: "Doctor, I suffer from premature ejaculation. Can you help?" **Doctor:** "No, but I can introduce you to a woman with a short attention span..."

•••••

A man suffering from premature ejaculation goes to his doctor. The doctor suggests that he tries to startle himself when he's about to ejaculate because this might solve the problem. The man buys a starter pistol, runs home and finds his wife naked in the bedroom. Losing no time, they start having sex. The next day the man goes back to the doctor. "How did it go?" asks the doctor. "Not too good," the man replies. "We were in the 69 position. I felt myself coming, so I fired the gun. Then my wife shit on my face, bit three inches off my penis and my neighbor ran out of the closet with his hands in the air!"

Prison

An accountant is sent to jail for embezzlement. They put him in a cell with a huge evil-looking guy. The big guy says, "I want to have some sex. You wanna be the husband or the wife?" The accountant replies, "Well, if I have to be one or the other, I guess I'd rather be the husband." The big guy replies, "Okay. Now get over here and suck your wife's dick..."

• • • • •

What do prisons and women have in common? They're both easier to get into the second time around.

Professional Ladies

A beautiful woman sits next to a drunk in a bar. He turns to her and says, "Hey, honey. How about you and me getting it on? I've got a couple dollars and it looks like you could use the money." The woman turns to him and asks, "What makes you think I charge by the inch?"

• • • • •

A boy and his date are parked on a country road, making out in his car. Suddenly the girl stops the boy, "I really should have mentioned this earlier," she says. "But I'm actually a hooker and I charge $20 for sex." The boy pays her and they do their thing. After they've finished the girl asks to go home and the boy requests his fare. "What d'you mean, fare?" "Well, I should have mentioned this earlier," says the boy. "But I'm actually a taxi driver and the fare back to town is $25!"

•••••

A class of children is asked what their parents do for a living. Little Johnny sticks up his hand and says, "My mommy's a substitute." The teacher knows that Little Johnny's mother works in a whorehouse so she corrects him. "I'm sorry," says the teacher. "But you mother isn't a substitute, she's a prostitute." "No," replies Johnny. "My *sister's* a prostitute, but when she can't make it into work my mommy is the substitute!"

•••••

A cowboy walks into a saloon and says, "I hear Big Bella, the roughest, toughest meanest whore this side of the Colorado, works here." "She sure does," replies the bartender. "Upstairs, first door on the right." The cowboy buys two bottles of beer and runs up the stairs to Big Bella's room. He bursts in and asks, "Are you Big Bella, the roughest, toughest, meanest whore this side of the Colorado?" "I sure am," replies Bella, who then lifts her skirts, lies back on the bed and grabs her ankles. "Don't you want a drink first?" asks the cowboy. "Why d'you think I'm lying like this?" asks Bella, "Hurry up and get the caps off them bottles!"

•••••

A man goes to a Bangkok bar, but is told that no girls are available. "We do have a pig though," says the madam. "She very popular—you can have her for half price." The man thinks he might as well, so he pays up and is shown into a room with a sow in it. He has sex and enjoys the experience so much he returns the next day. "Sorry," says the madam. "No pig today—why you not try special show? One of our girls is having sex with donkey." The man agrees and is shown into a darkened room that has a wall covered in peepholes. He looks through one and sees a girl having sex with a donkey. "Wow!" he says. "This is great." One of the other customers turns to him and says, "If you think this is good, you should have been here yesterday. They had this guy fucking a pig!"

• • • • •

A man goes to a brothel and says to the madam, "I want to get screwed." The madam tells him to go up to Room 12 and knock on the door. He walks up to the door, knocks on it and says, "I want to get screwed." A sexy voice replies, "Just slide $20 under the door." He slides the money under the door and waits, but nothing happens! So he knocks on the door again and says, "Hey! I want to get screwed!" The sexy voice replies, "Again?"

• • • • •

A man goes to a whorehouse and pays $20 to lick out a girl. The madam takes his money, gives him a girl and shows him to a room. He gets down to it, but is soon surprised to find a piece of broccoli in his mouth. The man spits out the broccoli only to discover he's also licked up a lump of carrot and a piece of potato. He looks up at the girl and says, "Excuse me, Miss, but you ain't sick, are you?" "No, I ain't," replies the girl. "But the last guy down there was!"

•••••

A man is out shopping with his wife and they decide to split up for a couple of hours. As the man wanders around, he spots a prostitute on a street corner. He goes over to see what she charges. "It's $50 for full sex," says the prostitute. "$25 for a blow job and $5 for a hand job." The man checks his pockets and finds he only has $3 in cash. "You won't get much for that," warns the prostitute, "and certainly nothing from me!" Later, the man and his wife are walking back to their car. The prostitute spots him from over the road and shouts, "Hey! I said you wouldn't get much for $3!"

•••••

A man is sitting in a bar when an exceptionally gorgeous young woman enters. She's so striking the man can't take his eyes off her. The woman notices his attentive stare and walks over. "I can see you're interested," says the woman. "So tell you what, I'll do anything you want me to do for $100, but there's one condition..." "What's that?" stammers the man. The woman replies, "You have to tell me what you want me to do in just three words." "And you'll do absolutely anything I want?" asks the man. "Anything," she replies. The man thinks for a moment then takes $100 out of his wallet. He gives her the money, looks into her eyes and says, "Paint my house."

•••••

A man walks up to a prostitute and asks how much she charges for a hand job. "$100," she replies. "That's a bit much, isn't it?" the man remarks. "See that Porsche parked over there?" says the prostitute. "I own that car because I give the best hand jobs in town." The man decides to take the hand job and enjoys it so much he asks how much she charges for oral sex. "$250," she replies. "Now that's really expensive," says the man. The prostitute points at a boat on the river. "See that speedboat?" she says. "I was able to pay for that in cash because I give the best oral in town." Impressed, the man pays for the oral. The sex is terrific, so the man asks the prostitute how much it costs to screw her. She points at a luxury apartment block. "You see those buildings?" she says. "Wow!" exclaims the man. "You mean you *own* that whole block?" "No," says the prostitute. "But I would if I had a pussy!"

• • • • •

A prostitute catches a cab home. When they arrive outside her apartment the cabbie asks for his fare. The woman sits back, hitches up her skirt and opens her legs. "I got a suggestion," she says. "How about you take *this* as payment?" The cabbie replies, "Have you got anything smaller?"

• • • • •

A sex researcher calls a survey participant to check on a discrepancy. "Sir," asks the researcher. "In response to the question on frequency of intercourse you answered 'twice weekly.' Your wife, on the other hand, answered 'several times a night.'" "That's right," the man replies, "And that's how it's going to be until the mortgage is paid off!"

• • • • •

A teenage girl becomes a prostitute, but on her first day at the brothel it's raided and everyone is forced to stand out in the street while the police take their details. The girl is horrified to see her grandmother walking toward her and tries to hide, but the old lady sees her. "Hello, dear," says the old lady. "What are you lining up for?" "Oh," says the granddaughter. "Er, we're, um, just waiting to get some oranges. They're handing out free samples." "Really?" says grandma. "Well, I think I'll get some of those myself." At that moment a cop comes by and spots the old woman. "Aren't you a bit old to be standing out here?" he asks. "I'm very fit for my age," says the old lady. "But how do you manage?" asks the cop. "Well," she replies. "Usually I just pop out my teeth and suck 'em dry!"

•••••

A tourist in Sweden is drinking in a bar when an attractive woman sits next to him. "Hello," he says. "Do you speak English?" "Oh, I speaking not much English," replies the woman. "How much?" asks the man. The woman replies, "200 kroner!"

•••••

A woman walks into an accountant's office to get help filing her taxes. The accountant asks the woman's occupation. "I'm a high-priced whore," says the woman. "No," the accountant exclaims. "That'll never work! Let's try to rephrase that." The woman says, "How about 'high-class call-girl'?" "That's still a little crude," says the accountant. "Can you think of anything else?" The woman thinks then says, "Why not 'elite chicken farmer.'" "Elite chicken farmer?" says the accountant. "What's that got to do with prostitution?" "Not much," the woman replies. "But I did raise over 5,000 little peckers last year!"

•••••

An old lady walks into a psychiatrist's office. "Doctor," she says. "I think I might be a nymphomaniac." "I might be able to help you," replies the psychiatrist. "But I should warn you that I charge $100 an hour." "That's reasonable," the old lady replies. "But how much for the whole night?"

•••••

An old sailor is in a brothel trying to make love with one of the girls. "How am I doing?" he asks. "Three knots," replies the girl. "What d'you mean, 'three knots'?" he asks. The girl replies, "You're not hard, you're not in and you're not getting your money back!"

•••••

I saw a woman standing by the road the other day. She said, "I'll spank you for $20." Straight away I called my mother and I said, "Mom, you could make a lot of money out here!"

•••••

What did the man say to the prostitute? "It's a business doing pleasure with you."

•••••

One Monday evening a tourist visits a brothel in Paris. He has a good time and, on leaving, he's very surprised to be handed 5,000 Euros. The next evening he goes back and the same thing happens again. He goes back on the third night, but doesn't get a single centime. Upset, he complains to the concierge. "Why should we pay you?" asks the concierge. "We don't film on Wednesdays!"

•••••

Three prostitutes—a mother, daughter and a grandmother—all live together. One night the daughter comes home looking upset. "How did you do tonight, dear?" asks the mother. "Not good," replies the daughter. "I only got a lousy $20 for a blow job." "$20!" exclaims the mother, "You should be grateful. In my day we gave a blow job for 50 cents!" "50 cents!" exclaims the grandmother. "You should be grateful. Back in the Depression, we were happy to get a hot meal!"

•••••

Two drunks are standing outside a whorehouse. The first drunk says, "I heard half these whores have the clap, the other half have crabs and none of them would think twice about stealing every penny we've got." "Shhhhh!" says the second drunk. "Not so loud, or they won't let us in!"

•••••

Two men visit a prostitute. The first man goes into the bedroom. Ten minutes later he comes out and says, "Heck, my wife is better than that!" The second man goes in. He comes out ten minutes later and says, "Know what? Your wife *is* better!"

•••••

Why is a prostitute luckier than a drug dealer? A prostitute can reuse her crack after she sells it!

Professional Ladies: Not So Professional

A couple are having financial problems so it's decided that the wife should turn to prostitution to make some extra cash. After her first night on the streets the woman returns home and empties her bag onto the kitchen table. Her husband counts the take. "There's two hundred dollars and fifty cents in here," he remarks. "That's not bad, but who on earth gave you the fifty cents?" His wife replies, "Well, *all* of them!"

• • • • •

A married couple fall on hard times. They decide that the only way they can keep the wolf from the door is if the wife becomes a prostitute. The wife decides to work from home and, after putting an ad in the paper, she gets her first client. She takes the man upstairs and he asks her how much she charges for full sex. The wife doesn't have a clue, so she runs downstairs, where her husband is waiting in the kitchen. "Charge him $70 for full sex," he tells her. Back upstairs the wife tells the man the cost, but he says he only has $20. The wife runs downstairs and asks her husband what she should give him for $20. "Tell him he can have a blow job for that," says the husband. The wife runs upstairs again and tells her customer what he can expect for $20. He starts to strip. He removes his pants and underwear, and the wife is astonished at the huge size of his erect member. She runs downstairs and says to her husband, "Hey, you couldn't lend us $50, could you?"

Pubic Hair

How do women get rid of unwanted pubic hairs? They spit them out!

• • • • •

What do parsley and pubic hair have in common? You always push them to one side and keep on eating!

Rednecks

What has six boobs and three teeth? The night shift at an Arkansas Waffle House!

• • • • •

Why do rednecks prefer sex "doggy style"? It means they can both watch the wrestling on TV.

• • • • •

A redneck goes to see his doctor. He pulls down his pants to reveal a beaten-up, bruised and bleeding penis. "Jesus! What happened to that?" asks the doctor. The redneck says, "Well, I live in a trailer park and I noticed that the woman in the next door trailer has a small hole in her wall. I also seen how most nights she sticks a hot dog in that hole and uses it to screw herself. Now I reckoned that I could do a better job, so last night I pulled that hot dog out and I stuck in my dick." "And did she notice the difference?" asks the doctor. "No, sir," the redneck replies. "In fact, we was doing great until someone knocked on her door. That's when she pulls down her dress, jumps off ma' dick and tries to kick it under the oven."

•••••

A reporter gets a job on an Arkansas newspaper and is told to find some human interest stories. He goes into the countryside, finds a remote farmhouse deep in the woods and asks the farmer if he knows of any heart-warming tales. "Well," says the farmer. "One time a neighbor lost one of his sheep. We all formed a posse and found it. And, after we had all screwed that sheep, we took it back to the farmer that done lost it." "I can't print a story like that," says the reporter. "Haven't you got any other heart-warming tales?" "Well, sure," says the farmer. "One time the daughter of ma' neighbor got lost, so we all formed a posse and found her. And, after all of us had screwed her, we took that lost gal right back to her daddy." "That's disgusting," says the reporter. "I can't print that! Look, forget heart-warming—have you got any tales that are tragic?" The farmer hangs his head and a tear trickles down his cheek. "Well," he says. "There was this one time when *I* got lost..."

•••••

How does a redneck mother know when her daughter is having her period? Her son's dick tastes funny!

•••••

Billy-Bob comes home early and finds his wife, Mary, lying naked on the bed, dying of a heart attack. He picks up the phone to call the doctor when his young son shouts out, "Dad! There's a nude man in the closet!" Billy-Bob opens the closet door and finds his best friend naked inside. "I don't believe it!" he shouts, "Mary's dying on the bed and you're playing games with the damn kids!"

• • • • •

Billy-Bob goes up to Joe and says, "Hey, d'you like women with big sagging titties and hairy nipples?" "No," replies Joe. "And do you like women with pimply backsides and stretch-marked stomachs?" continues Billy-Bob. "No," replies Joe. "And do you like women with VD and yeast infections?" "Jesus! No, I don't!" replies Joe. "Good," says Billy-Bob. "Then you won't mind staying the hell away from my wife!"

• • • • •

Billy-Bob is walking down the street with some chicken wire under his arm. Leroy asks him what he's doing. "It's chicken wire," says Billy-Bob. "I'm going to use it to catch some chickens." "You fool," says Leroy. "You can't catch chickens with chicken wire." But later that day Leroy sees Billy-Bob dragging a net full of chickens down the road. The next day Billy-Bob is walking down the street with some duct tape under his arm. Leroy asks what he's doing. "I got me some duct tape," says Billy-Bob. "I'm going to use it to catch some ducks." "You fool," says Leroy. "You can't catch ducks with duct tape." But later that day Leroy sees Billy-Bob dragging a net full of ducks down the road. The next day Billy-Bob is walking down the street with some sticks under his arm. Leroy says, "What you got there?" Billy-Bob replies, "Pussy willow." Leroy says, "I'll get my hat…"

• • • • •

Cletus decides to give his wife, Missy-Sue, a treat for their wedding anniversary. He buys 24 bottles of champagne and pours them into a tub so she can have a real fancy bubble bath. After she's finished, Cletus decides to be thrifty and carefully pours all the champagne back into the bottles. He gets to the last bottle, fills it and finds there's still a pint of champagne left in the tub. He calls out into the bedroom, "Dang-it, Missy! Why the hell did yus have ta piss in it?!"

• • • • •

How do you circumcise a hillbilly? Kick his sister under the chin!

• • • • •

Joe sees Billy-Bob walking around town with nothing on except his boots. "Billy-Bob," says Joe. "What the hell you doin' walking around town naked?" Billy-Bob replies, "Well, Joe, Mary-Lou and me was down on the farm and we started a-kissing. Mary-Lou then says we should go to the barn, so we did. Inside the barn we starts a-kissing and a-cuddling, and things got pretty hot and heavy. Then Mary-Lou says we should go up in the hayloft. So we gets up there and Mary-Lou takes off all her clothes and says I should do likewise. So I takes off all my clothes except my boots. Then Mary-Lou lays on the hay, opens her legs wide open and says, 'Okay, Billy-Bob, go to town...'"

• • • • •

Three hillbillies are walking down the road when they see a pig's ass sticking out of a bush. The first hillbilly says, "Gosh, I'm so horny—I sure wish that were Demi Moore's ass." The second hillbilly says, "Gosh, I'm so horny—I sure wish that were Dolly Parton's ass." The third hillbilly says, "Gosh, I'm right horny too—I wish this was nighttime!"

•••••

Three rednecks are sitting on a porch comparing wives. The first redneck says, "My Cindy's so dumb, she bought a toilet and we don't even have running water." The second says, "That's nothing! My Maisie bought a ceiling fan and we don't even have no electricity." The third says, "Aw, that 'taint nothing! I was goin' through my Lou-Lou's purse for some whisky money and I found a box of condoms. And you know what? She ain't even got a dick!"

•••••

What does it mean when a woman from West Virginia has sperm running out of both sides of her mouth? The trailer's level!

Religion

A bus full of nuns crashes and the sisters find themselves lining up at the Pearly Gates. Saint Peter interviews them as they pass through the portal. To the first nun he says, "Sister, did you ever touch a penis during your time as a nun?" "Only once,. your eminence," replies the first nun. "When I was a nurse I touched one with the tips of my fingers." "I see," says Saint Peter. "In that case dip your fingers in the holy water and you may pass into Heaven." He then poses the same question to the second nun, who replies, "I did touch a penis, sir." "When I was a nurse one rubbed against my wrist." Saint Peter replies, "In that case, dab the holy water on your wrist and you may enter the Kingdom of Heaven." At that moment Saint Peter notices a fight breaking out farther down the line. "What's going on down there?" he demands. One of the nuns shouts back, "I want to get in line before Sister Mary! If I've got to gargle that stuff, I want to do it before she sticks her ass in it!"

•••••

A chaplain is walking through a notorious section of town when he sees a soldier leaving a brothel. The soldier pauses on the sidewalk and gestures with his right hand in a manner familiar to the good Catholic chaplain. The chaplain approaches the soldier, saying, "I'm sorry to see a good Catholic lad like you coming out of a place like that." "I'm not Catholic," answers the soldier. "But I saw you cross yourself," the chaplain continues. "Listen, Padre," says the soldier. "When I come out of a place like that, I always check four things—my spectacles, my testicles, my watch and my wallet!"

•••••

A journalist goes to Afghanistan and is surprised to see that the local men allow their wives to walk in front of them. He approaches a local and remarks, "I thought the custom in Islamic countries was for wives to walk ten paces behind their husbands?" "It was," replies the local. "But that all changed with the war." "How did the war change things?" asks the journalist. The local replies, "Landmines!"

•••••

A nun and a priest are riding a camel through the desert. After a few days the camel drops dead and the pair realize they're doomed. The priest says, "Our time on earth will be short. Sister, could I ask a favor? I have never in my life seen a pair of woman's breasts—could I see yours?" The nun agrees and reveals her breasts. "May I touch them?" asks the priest. The nun agrees and the priest has a feel. The nun then says, "Father, I too would like to ask a favor. I have never seen a man's penis before—would you show me yours?" The priest agrees and exposes himself. "And may I touch it, Father?" asks the nun. The priest agrees and the nun has a fondle. Not surprisingly the priest develops a huge erection. "Y'know," he says. "If I put my penis in the proper place, it can give life." "Holy Mother!" exclaims the nun. "Why did you not say so before? Stick it up that camel's asshole and let's get the fuck out of here!"

•••••

A nun gets into a cab. After a few minutes the cab driver says, "I hope you won't be offended, but it's always been a fantasy of mine to have a nun perform oral sex on me." The nun replies, "That could be arranged, but only on two conditions: You must be a Catholic and you must be single." The cab driver says, "Well, I'm both! I'm single and I'm Catholic, too!" "Okay," says the nun. "Pull over." The cab driver pulls over and the nun fulfills his fantasy. When they get back on the road, the driver says, "Thanks for that, but I ought to confess: I'm not single and I'm not Catholic. I'm a married Protestant." The nun replies, "That's alright. I ought to confess too: My name's Thomas. I'm on my way to a costume party!"

•••••

A priest in a small Irish village has a cock and ten hens, which he keeps in a hen house behind the church. One

Saturday night the cock goes missing and the priest suspects it's been stolen. During Mass the next day, the priest questions his congregation, "Has anybody got a cock?" he asks. All the men stand up. "No, no!" he says, "What I meant to say was, has anybody *seen* a cock?" Everyone stands up. "No, no!" says the priest, "What I should have said was, has anybody seen a cock that doesn't belong to them?" Half the women stand up. "No, no!" says the priest, "What I'm trying to say is, who here has seen *my* cock?" All the nuns, three altar boys and a goat stand up!

• • • • •

A trainee priest is hearing confessions when one of the parishioners admits to an act of sodomy. The priest can't remember what the penance for this sin should be, so he beckons over one of the altar boys. "What does Father O'Neill usually give for sodomy?" whispers the priest. The boy whispers back, "A chocolate ice cream cone and a Coke."

• • • • •

A vicar visits a young man in his parish and discovers that a party is in full swing. All the guests are blindfolded, naked men and they're playing a game where they try to guess identities by fondling each other's genitals. "Oh, dear," says the vicar. "I'd better go—this isn't my cup of tea at all." "Rubbish," says the young man. "Your name's been called out three times already!"

• • • • •

An elderly Italian man goes to confession. "Father," he says. "I'd like to ask you a question." "Certainly, my son," says the priest. "During the war a beautiful Jewish woman knocked on my door," says the old man. "And she asked me to hide her in return for sexual favors." "That was wrong of you," the priest replies. "You shouldn't have taken advantage of the woman, but you did a good deed in saving her life. Say fifty Hail Marys." "No, Father," says the old man. "That wasn't the question." "Then what *is* your question?" the priest asks. The old man says, "Do I have to tell her the war is over?"

• • • • •

Father O'Reilly is having a quiet jack-off session in the cathedral vestry when a tourist spots him and takes a picture. "Oh, my God!" cries the Father. "That picture must never be seen. How much d'you want for that camera?" "Five hundred dollars," says the tourist. This is an extortionate amount but the Father has no choice, so he pays up. Later, Sister Mary sees him with his new camera. "That's very nice, Father," says Sister Mary. "How much did you buy it for?" "Five hundred dollars," Father O'Reilly replies. "Christ!" exclaims the Sister. "Someone must've seen you coming!"

• • • • •

How can you tell when you enter a gay church? Only half the congregation are on their knees!

• • • • •

How do you get a nun pregnant? Dress her up as an altar boy.

• • • • •

I was waiting at a red light when I saw that the car in front had a bumper sticker that read, "Honk if you love Jesus."

So I honked. The driver leaned out his window, gave me the finger and yelled, "Can't you see the light is still red, you fucking moron?"

·····

Sister Anne goes into a liquor store and asks for a bottle of vodka. "It's for the Mother Superior," she explains. "It's to relieve her constipation." An hour later the shopkeeper is closing up for the night when he hears noises coming from a nearby alley. He looks up the alley and sees Sister Anne sitting dead drunk in a pool of vomit and urine. "Sister Anne!" he exclaims. "You said that drink was to help the Reverend Mother's constipation!" "It is," slurs the Sister. "When she hears about this, she's going to shit herself!"

·····

Three trainee priests line up for a celibacy test. The first trainee goes into a room, strips and has a bell tied to his penis. A nude pole dancer then does her act for him and the inevitable happens—he gets excited and the bell goes "ting-a-ling-a-ling." "I'm sorry," says the head priest. "You don't have the strength of character to be a priest. Now go and take a shower." The second candidate enters the room, strips and has a bell tied on. But again, when the pole dancer goes into her act the bell goes "ting-a-ling-a-ling." "I'm sorry," says the head priest. "You're not up to the job— go and take a shower." The third candidate enters the room, strips and has the bell put on him. When the pole dancer appears he watches her with no reaction, no matter how hard she tries to arouse him. Eventually she gives up and the head priest walks over to congratulate the trainee, "Well done, my son! You showed remarkable forbearance.

You're just what the church is looking for. Now go and join the other lads in the shower…'ting-a-ling-a-ling.'"

Revenge

A husband comes home to find his wife in bed with another man. He drags the man into the garage and puts his dick in a vice. He then secures the vice tightly, removes the handle and picks up a hacksaw. Terrified, the man screams, "Stop! For God's sakes, don't cut it off! Don't cut it off!" The husband hands the man the hacksaw and says, "I'm not the one who's cutting it off—I'm the one setting fire to the garage!"

•••••

Bill is a soldier stationed abroad. His wife finds out he's been cheating on her, so she sends him a "special" package: a box of home-baked cookies and a Clint Eastwood movie on tape. Bill is delighted with the gifts and invites some friends over to watch the movie and eat cookies. They're sitting on a couch, enjoying themselves, when Bill's wife suddenly appears on the TV screen. She's on her knees, giving a guy a blow job. The guy shoots his load and Bill's wife spits his mess into a bowl of cookie dough. "Hi, Bill," she says to the camera. "I want a divorce…"

•••••

John and Joe are about to tee off on the golf course when a stranger asks if he can join them. Being friendly types, they let him and the conversation soon turns to professions. The stranger reveals that he's a hitman and is actually carrying his gun in his golf bag. John doesn't believe him and asks to see it. Sure enough, inside the golf bag is a rifle with a huge telescopic sight. Joe asks if he can look through it. "Wow!" says Joe, "I can see my house with this. Look, there's my bedroom window! I can even see my wife sitting on the bed." Suddenly he turns pale. "Oh, my God! She's in there with our neighbor and they're both stark naked." Furious, Joe turns to the hitman and asks, "Okay, how much to shoot my lying wife in the mouth and my cheating neighbor in the dick?" The hitman replies, "I get five thousand dollars every time I pull the trigger." "It's a deal," says Joe. "Do it now!" The hitman picks up his rifle, takes aim and waits. A few seconds pass. "Why don't you shoot?" asks Joe, "Shhh!" says the hitman. "I'm trying to save you five thousand bucks!"

Riddle Me Ree

How do get a pound of meat out of a fly? Unzip it.

How do you make a skeleton? Hose down a leper.

How do you turn a fox into an elephant? Marry it!

If the dove is the Bird of Peace, what is the Bird of True Love? The swallow!

What are the four words most hated by men during sex? "Is it in yet?"

What are the four words most hated by women during sex? "Hi, honey! I'm home!"

What do gay men call hemorrhoids? Speed bumps!

What do women and police cars have in common? They both make a lot of noise to let you know they're coming.

What do you call a guy with a one-inch dick? Justin!

What do you call a fat girl with a yeast infection? A Whopper with cheese!

What do you call a room full of women with PMS and yeast infections? A whine & cheese party.

What do you call a 300-pound person who likes sex with males and females? A bisexual built for two.

What do you call a vegetarian with diarrhea? A salad shooter!

What do you call an Eskimo lesbian? A Klondyke.

What do you call kids born in a whorehouse? Brothel sprouts!

What do you call kinky sex with chocolate? S&M&M.

What do you call ten naked men sitting on each other's shoulders? A scrotum pole!

What do you call two skunks doing a 69? Odor-Eaters!

What goes "Click—is that it? Click—is that it? Click—is that it?" A blind person with a Rubik's cube!

What has one hundred teeth and holds back a huge monster? My zipper!

What kind of bee makes milk? A boo-bee.

What part of a woman does a man like looking at best? The top of her head!

What should you do if your girlfriend starts smoking? Slow down… and possibly use a lubricant.

What's better than a rose on your piano? Tulips on your organ!

What's black and crispy and comes on a stick? Joan of Arc.

What's black, has long ears and smokes? A rabbit chewing a power cable.

What's blue and screws supermodels? Me, in my lucky blue coat!

What's the fastest thing on two legs? An Ethiopian with a luncheon voucher.

What's 14 inches long and has an asshole behind it? George Bush's tie.

What's blue and fucks old ladies? Hypothermia.

What's brown and sits on a piano bench? Beethoven's first movement.

What's good on a pizza, but bad on a pussy? A crust.

What's green and yellow and eats nuts? Gonorrhea.

What's red and white and sits in trees? A sanitary owl.

What's short and straight to the point? A midget nymphomaniac!

What's soft and warm when you go to bed, but hard and stiff when you wake up? Vomit!

What's the definition of self-destruction? An epileptic leper!

What's the difference between "Oooh!" and "Aaah!"? About three inches!

What's the toughest part of a man's body? His cock—it can stand up to any cunt!

What's white and 14 inches long? Absolutely nothing!

What's white, sits by the bed and takes the piss out of you? A dialysis machine.

Why can't gypsies have babies? Because their husbands have crystal balls.

Why is it called sex? Because it's easier to spell than "Uhhhhh... Oooohh, Ahhhhhh... AIIEEEEEEE!"

What's 10 inches long, 2 inches thick and starts with a "P"? A really good crap.

What's the difference between purple and pink? The grip.

What's the definition of disappointment? You get the stool lined up and the cow walks off.

What's the best way to get into a sleeping bag? Wake her up first!

Why is a sheep better than a woman? A sheep doesn't care if you screw her sister.

Sales and Retail

A woman goes into a hardware shop to buy a hinge. She takes it to the counter and the clerk says, "Want a screw for that hinge?" "No," replies the woman. "But I'll suck you off for a toaster!"

• • • • •

Betty and Jane are shopping together at the supermarket. When they get to the vegetables, Betty reaches into a sack of potatoes and takes out two big ones. "You know, Jane, these remind me of my husband's balls." "Wow!" says Jane. "Are they that big?" "No," replies Betty. "They're that dirty!"

• • • • •

A woman has just started a new job on the supermarket checkout when the manager comes over to tell her about "product linking." "What's product linking?" she asks. "I'll demonstrate with the next customer," says the boss. Along comes the next customer and among his items, he has a bag of grass seed. The manager says, "sir, I see you have a bag of grass seed in your shopping—have you considered buying a lawnmower? We have some on special offer at

$49.99." "What a good idea," says the customer. "I'll take one." The checkout girl is impressed. Along comes the next customer and among his items, he has a box of Tampax. The checkout girl says, "sir, I see you have a box of Tampax for your girlfriend in your shopping—have you considered buying a lawnmower? We have some on special offer at $49.99." "What's a lawnmower got to do with Tampax?" asks the customer. The girl replies, "Well, your weekend's fucked anyway, so I thought you might as well mow the lawn!"

• • • • •

A glamorous woman is doing her shopping at the supermarket. She gets to the checkout and notices that the person bagging up her purchases is an extremely handsome young man. "Could you take my bags to my car?" she asks. "Certainly, madam," replies the young man. The woman leans toward him and winks, "Y'know," she says. "I have an itchy pussy." "Well, you'll have to show me," replies the man. "All these Japanese cars look the same to me!"

• • • • •

A man is at the supermarket checkout when he realizes he's forgotten to pick up condoms. He asks the checkout girl if she can have someone bring a packet over. "Sure," says the girl, "but I'll have to check your size." With that, she sticks her hands down the man's pants and fiddles around. She then shouts out, "One box of large condoms to Checkout 10!" The next man in line sees this and decides he'd like to be felt up in the same way. When he gets to the checkout, he also asks for some condoms to be sent over. So the girl sticks her hand down his pants, has a quick rummage and shouts out, "One box of medium condoms to Checkout 10!" The next customer in line is a teenage boy. He decides to pull the same trick and also asks for condoms. The girl sticks her hands down his pants, has a feel around and shouts, "Clean-up crew to Checkout 10!"

•••••

A man is walking around a supermarket shouting, "Mazola! Mazola!" The manager comes up to him and says, "Excuse me, sir, the Mazola is in aisle five." "I'm not really looking for Mazola," says the man. "I'm calling my wife." "I see," says the manager. "Your wife's name is 'Mazola'?" "It's sort of a nickname," says the man. "But I only call her that in public." "And what do you call her at home?" inquires the manager. The man replies, "Lard ass!"

•••••

A store owner hires a young female clerk who likes to wear very short skirts. One day a man enters the store and orders some raisin bread. The raisin bread is on the very top shelf and the girl has to climb a ladder to get it—giving the man a great view up her skirt. Others notice this and pretty soon there's a line of men waiting to order raisin bread. The clerk is getting annoyed at having to go up and down the ladder all the time. She looks down and sees an old man joining the end of the line. The girl shouts to him, "Hey! Is yours raisin too?" "No," croaks the old man. "But it sure is startin' to twitch!"

•••••

Morris gets a job selling toothbrushes but doesn't do very well. Lance, on the other hand, is the top salesman selling thousands of toothbrushes every week. Morris gets desperate and asks Lance for the secret of his success. After much pleading Lance agrees to divulge his method. He opens a box and gets out a large pot of brown sludge and a plate of crackers. "What I do," says Lance, "is take this pot to the airport with a big sign saying 'Free crackers and dip,' then I tell passengers to help themselves." "How does that help you sell toothbrushes?" asks Morris. "Try it yourself," says Lance. So Morris takes a cracker and uses it to scoop some dip in his mouth. It tastes awful and he spits it out. "Oh, my God!" he shouts, "It tastes like crap!" "It *is* crap," replies Lance. "Want to buy a toothbrush?"

• • • • •

A man gets a job at a sex shop. The shop is having a dildo sale and a young blonde walks in and asks to see the dildos on special offer. "We have black ones and white ones on sale," says the man. "They're the same size and the same price: $15." "Well, I've already got some black dildos and some white ones," says the blonde. "How about that tartan one on the shelf?" "That's a special model," says the man. "It's not on sale and it costs $250." "Wow!" says the blonde. "It's expensive, but I've never seen a tartan one before. Y'know, I'll take it!" So the man wraps up the tartan dildo and the blonde pays for it and leaves. A short while later the man's boss comes back from lunch. "Sold any of those $15 dildos?" he asks. "No," replies the man. "But I just let your thermos go for $250!"

• • • • •

A lady walks into a shop selling expensive Persian rugs. She bends over to inspect one of the rugs and farts loudly.

Embarrassed, she looks around to see if anyone has noticed her. All of a sudden a salesman pops up behind her. "Good day, madam," he says. "And how may I help you?" "What's the price of this lovely rug?" asks the woman. The salesman starts laying down sheets of newspaper on the floor. "What on earth are you doing?" asks the woman. The salesman replies, "Madam, if you farted just looking at it, you'll shit yourself when I tell you how much it costs!"

Santa Claus

A beautiful young girl wants to meet Santa Claus so she puts on a robe and stays up late on Christmas Eve. Santa arrives, climbs down the chimney and unloads his presents. He's about to leave when the girl says, "Oh, Santa, please stay. Keep the chill away." Santa replies, "Ho, ho, ho! Gotta go, gotta go! Gotta get the presents to the children, you know." The girl drops her robe to reveal her underwear and says, "Oh, Santa. Don't run a mile, just stay for a while..." Santa begins to sweat, but replies, "Ho, ho, ho! Gotta go, gotta go! Gotta get the presents to the children, you know." The girl takes off her bra and says, "Oh, Santa, please stay..." Santa wipes his brow and replies, "Ho, ho, ho! Gotta go, gotta go! Gotta get the presents to the children, you know." The girl takes off her panties and says, "Oh, Santa, please stay..." Santa says, "Hey, hey, hey! Gotta stay, gotta stay! Can't get up that chimney with my pecker this way!"

•••••

Why is Santa's sack so big? He only comes once a year.

School and Education

Jimmy applies for a scholarship to an expensive private school. As part of the entrance exam he's asked a series of questions by the school principal and a teacher, Ms. Brooks. "What does a cow have four of, that I have only two of?" asks Ms. Brooks. Jimmy replies, "Legs." Ms. Brooks asks, "What's in your pants that you have, but I don't?" Jimmy answers, "Pockets." Ms. Brooks asks, "What does a dog do that a man steps into?" Jimmy replies, "Pants." Ms. Brooks asks, "What starts with a 'C' and ends with a 'T,' is hairy and oval?" Jimmy replies, "A coconut." Ms. Brooks asks, "What goes in hard and pink, then comes out soft and sticky?" Jimmy answers, "Bubblegum." Ms. Brooks asks, "What does a man do standing up, a woman do sitting down and a dog do on three legs?" Jimmy replies, "Shake hands." Ms. Brooks asks, "You stick your poles inside me, you tie me down to get me up, I get wet before you do... What am I?" Jimmy replies, "A tent." Ms. Brooks asks, "A finger goes in me, you fiddle with me when you're bored, the best man always has me first... What am I?" Jimmy replies, "A wedding ring." Ms. Brooks asks, "I come in many sizes... When I'm not well, I drip... When you blow me, you feel good... What am I?" Jimmy replies, "A nose." Ms. Brooks asks, "I have a stiff shaft, my tip penetrates, I come with a quiver... What am I?" Jimmy replies, "An arrow." Ms. Brooks asks, "What word starts with an 'F' and ends in 'K' that means a lot of heat and excitement?" Jimmy replies, "A firetruck." After the test Ms. Brooks turns to the principal and asks, "Well, how did he do?" The principal replies, "Great! The boy's a genius—I got the last ten wrong myself…"

• • • • •

A boy comes home from school and tells his father that he fell out of the class spelling competition in the first round. "What word did they give you?" asks his father. The boy replies, "Posse." His father laughs, "I'm not surprised you can't *spell* it—you can't even *pronounce* it!"

• • • • •

A lecturer is giving his medical class a lesson in observation. He holds up a jar of yellow liquid. "To be a doctor, you have to be observant," he explains. "Observant of color, smell, sight and taste." The lecturer then dips his finger into the jar and puts his finger in his mouth. His students watch in disgust but when the jar is passed round they all do the same and grimace at the horrible taste. When the jar is back on his desk the lecturer says, "Congratulations! The observant among you will have noticed that I put my second finger into the jar and my index finger in my mouth!"

• • • • •

A teacher explains the word "definitely" to her class and asks them to make up a sentence using the word. A pupil raises her hand and says, "The sky is definitely blue." The teacher replies, "That's good, but sometimes the sky can also be gray." Another pupil says, "Grass is definitely green." The teacher says, "That's good too, but grass can also go brown." Little Johnny sticks up his hand and says, "Miss, do farts definitely have lumps?" Annoyed, the teacher says, "No! And just for that, you're not leaving this classroom until you use 'definitely' correctly." Little Johnny replies, "Well, in that case, I definitely just shit my pants!"

• • • • •

A teacher is telling her class about a big test the next day. "There's no excuse for being absent," she says, "barring a death in the family or a medical emergency." Smart-ass Johnny sticks his hand up: "What if I come in tomorrow suffering from extreme sexual exhaustion?" The class sniggers and teacher says, "That won't be a problem, Johnny—you can always write with your other hand!"

• • • • •

Antonio comes home from school and walks into the kitchen. His grandma says, "Antonio, what did you learn in school today?" Antonio replies, "We learned about penises and vaginas and sexual intercourse and masturbation." Grandma slaps Antonio hard and he runs crying to his room. His mother walks in and says, "Mama! Why did you go and hit Antonio?" Grandma replies, "I asked him what he learned in school today and he started talking about sex and masturbation." Mother replies, "That's what they learn—it's called sex education!" Grandma feels guilty about hitting the boy, so she goes to apologize. She opens his bedroom door and finds him jerking off furiously. "Antonio," she says. "When you've finished your homework, come downstairs and I'll get you some cake."

• • • • •

My classmates would copulate with anything that moved. But I never saw any reason to limit myself.

• • • • •

A teacher says to her class, "Who can tell me the meaning of 'indifferent'?" Little Johnny puts up his hand. "It means 'lovely,' miss." "Why d'you think that?" asks teacher. Johnny replies, "Because last night when I was in bed, I heard Mommy say, 'That's lovely,' and Daddy says, 'Yep, it's in different'!"

• • • • •

A teacher asks her class for a sentence with the word "beautiful" in it twice. First, she calls on Little Suzy, who responds with, "My father bought my mother a beautiful dress and she looked beautiful in it." "Very good, Suzy," replies the teacher. She then calls on Little Michael. "My mommy planned a beautiful banquet and it turned out beautifully," he says. "Excellent, Michael!" says the teacher, who then calls on Little Johnny. Little Johnny says, "Last night my sister told my father that she was pregnant and he said, 'Beautiful, fucking beautiful'!"

• • • • •

A teacher asks her class some questions, telling them that the first to answer can go home early. "Who said 'Four score and seven years ago'?" she says. Little Johnny sticks his hand up, but Little Pattie beats him to it, "Abraham Lincoln," she says. "Very good," replies the teacher. "You can go home. Now who said, 'I have a dream'?" Little Johnny puts his hand up, but is beaten by Little Mary. "Martin Luther King," she says. "Very good," replies the teacher. "You can go home. Now who said, 'Think not what your country can do for you'?" Little Johnny's hand shoots up, but he's beaten to it by Little Susie. "President

Kennedy," she says. "Very good," replies the teacher. "Jesus!" says Little Johnny. "I wish these fucking bitches would keep their mouths shut." "Who said that?" demands the teacher. "President Clinton!" shouts Little Johnny. "Now can I get the fuck out of here?"

• • • • •

A teacher asks Little Johnny to make up a sentence including the word "fascinate." Little Johnny thinks for a moment then says, "My sister has a red sweater with nine buttons on it, but her titties are so big she can only fasten eight!"

• • • • •

A teacher is playing a guessing game with her class. "What have I got behind my back?" asks the teacher. "I'll give you a clue—it's round, red and juicy." "A tomato?" asks Little Jenny. "No," says the teacher. "It's an apple, but I like the way you're thinking. Who can guess what I've got behind my back now? The clue is: It's small, green and hairy." "Is it a gooseberry?" asks Little Simon. "No," says the teacher. "It's a kiwi fruit, but I like the way you're thinking." Little Johnny sticks up his hand. "Miss, can you guess what I'm holding in my pocket?" "Give me a clue," says the teacher. Johnny replies, "Well, it's round, hard and has a head on it." "That's disgusting," says the teacher. "No," replies Johnny. "It's a coin, but I like the way you're thinking!"

• • • • •

A teacher says to her class, "Children, if you could have one element in the world, what would it be?" Little Jimmy says, "I'd want gold. With some gold, I could buy a Porsche." Little Sally says, "I'd want platinum. Platinum is worth more than gold and I could buy a Porsche and a Jaguar." Little Johnny says, "I'd want some silicone." "Silicone?" asks the teacher. "That's not very valuable, Johnny." "That's what you think," says Little Johnny. "My mom's got two bags of the stuff and you should see all the sports cars outside our house!"

•••••

A teacher walks into her classroom on Monday and sees that someone has written the word "penis" on the blackboard. She scans the class, looking for a guilty face, but there's no obvious suspect so she rubs the word off. The next day the same thing happens, except that the word "penis" is written in larger letters. Again, there's no obvious suspect so she rubs the word away. This goes on all week, and each day the word "penis" gets bigger and bigger on the board. Finally, the teacher comes into class on Friday and finds the word "penis" written in huge letters. Underneath is a caption reading, "Penis. The more you rub it the bigger it gets!"

•••••

The class is learning about nature when Little Johnny sticks his hand up. "Miss," he says. "Is it true that baby birds have spare parts?" "No," replies the teacher. "What ever gave you that idea?" "I heard my Dad and Uncle Billy talking," says Johnny. "And Uncle Billy said he'd really like to screw the ass off the chick next door!"

•••••

There's an English lesson at school: Each student has to stand up and speak a sentence using one spelling word.

Tommy's word is "love," so he gets up and says, "Sara says she loves me." Billy's word is "hate," so he gets up and says, "Sara says she hates me." Johnny's word is "dictate," so he gets up and says, "Sara says my dictate good!"

• • • • •

Why do drivers' education classes in redneck schools only use the car on Fridays? Because the rest of the week it's being used by Sex Ed.

• • • • •

Why don't Mexicans have driving lessons and sex education classes on the same day? Because it tires out the donkey!

Scottish

Two Scotsmen are walking through the woods when one ducks into the bushes to have a crap. After much grunting he finishes and calls out to his friend, "Alistair, have you got a piece o' paper?" His friend replies, "Don't be so tight-fisted, Hamish! Leave it where it is!"

• • • • •

Why do Scottish men wear kilts? Because sheep can hear a zipper a mile away!

Sex Change

A man goes into the hospital to have a circumcision. Unfortunately the hospital makes a mistake and he ends up having a complete sex change. When he wakes up the man goes to pieces and starts crying. "Oh, my God!" he moans. "I'll never be able to experience an erection again!" "Of course you will," says the surgeon. "It'll just have to be someone else's!"

• • • • •

Do you know the scientific name for a female sex change? A Strapadicktome.

Sex Problems

A woman goes to see her doctor. "I've got a problem," she says. "Every time we're in bed and my husband climaxes, he lets out this ear-splitting yell." "That's quite natural," replies the doctor. "I don't see what the problem is." The woman replies, "The problem is, it wakes me up!"

• • • • •

A man goes to his doctor and says, "I got this sex problem. It all starts in the middle of the night. My wife always wakes me up about three in the morning for nookie and then again about five so we can make love before I go to work." "I see…," says the doctor. "There's more," says the man. "When I get on the train to work I meet this girl every day. We get a compartment to ourselves and have sex all the way into town. Then I get to the office, where I have to give my secretary one in the storeroom." "I see…," says the doctor. "No, there's more," says the man. "When I go to lunch I meet this lady in the cafeteria and we sneak out the back for a quickie." "Now I understand…," says the doctor. "There's more," says the man. "When I get back to the office in the afternoon my female boss has to have me or she says she'll sack me." "Ahh...," says the doctor. "Now I see...," "No, there's more," says the man. "When I get home my wife is so pleased to see me she gives me a blow job before dinner and then we have sex till it's time to go to bed." "Okay," says the doctor. "Have you quite finished?" "Yes," says the man. "So what's your problem?" asks the doctor. "Well, y'see, Doc...," says the man. "It hurts when I masturbate!"

•••••

A psychiatrist is talking to a female patient about her sex life. "When you make love, do you ever look your husband in the face?" he asks. "I only did it once," replies the woman. "But he looked very angry." "And why do you think that was?" asks the psychiatrist. The woman replies, "Because he was looking in through the bedroom window!"

•••••

A woman goes to her doctor with inflamed knees. "Can you think of any reason why they might hurt?" asks the doctor. The woman replies, "My husband and I make love nine times a week and we always do it doggy style." "Well, there are other positions," replies the doctor. "Yes," says the woman. "But not if you want to watch TV!"

•••••

I tried fighting my sexual urges by taking cold showers. Now I get an erection every time it rains.

I haven't been the same since my testicles dropped—mind you, I was hanging from a tree by them at the time.

My doctor examined my testicles and found two small lumps. Luckily, it turned out they *were* my testicles.

How can you tell if your girlfriend's frigid? When you open her legs, the light goes on.

How can you tell if your girlfriend's frigid? When you open her legs, the central heating kicks in.

• • • • •

A young woman goes to her doctor with a bee up her vagina. The doctor tells her that the best chance of getting it out is if he dips his penis in honey and tries to lure it into the open. The woman agrees, so the doctor puts the tip of his honey-covered penis in the woman's vagina and waits. Nothing happens, so the doctor pushes it in a bit farther. Still nothing happens. The doctor pushes it all the way in, but still nothing happens. The doctor then goes red in the face and starts thrusting into his patient. "How's this going to tempt the bee?" asks the woman. "Change of plan," gasps the doctor. "We're going to drown it!"

• • • • •

My sex life isn't dead, but the buzzards are circling.

• • • • •

A man and a woman have sex. Afterward the woman says, "That was awful. You must be the worst lover in the world!" "That's ridiculous!" says the man. "How can you possibly say that after only ten seconds?"

Shoes

A newly married couple go to Morocco for their honeymoon. One day they're wandering through a market when they're invited into a shop selling slippers. They have a look at the wares, but can't see anything they like. They're just about to leave when Abdul the shopkeeper takes a pair of slippers from a high shelf. "Please, sir," he says. "Before you go, try on these special slippers. They have the magical ability to increase your sex drive. If you put these on, you will be insatiable. You will never tire of the sexual act." The couple are dubious, but to humor Abdul the man takes off his sandals and puts on the slippers. Immediately the man's eyes bulge out of their sockets. He gives a great roar, rips off his shorts, bends Abdul over a chair and tears off his robes. "No, no!" shouts Abdul. "Wrong feet! Wrong feet!"

Sick

A man starts a new job but phones in every Monday to say he's sick. Eventually his boss calls him in and asks, "Is there anything we can do for you? I'm sure we can find a cure for whatever illness you have." "Well, I'm not exactly ill," replies the man. "Y'see I like having sex with my mother, but Monday is the only day she has any free time." "What!" cries the boss. "You never come in Mondays because you're having sex with your mother?" "Hey," replies the man. "I told you I was sick!"

· · · · ·

Little Johnny is in church when he suddenly feels ill. "Run outside," says his mother, "and throw up in the bushes." A minute later Johnny is back, looking relieved. "Did you get to the bushes in time?" asks mother. "I didn't have to," replies Johnny. "I got to the door and found a box labeled 'For the Sick.'"

Skydiving

Did you hear about the female skydiver? She pulled the wrong string and bled to death.

Why do female skydivers wear jock straps? So they don't whistle on the way down!

• • • • •

A private is telling his girlfriend about his parachute training. "It was really scary," he says. "We were at 10,000 feet and I froze at the door. I couldn't do it, so the sergeant major came up behind me and said that if I didn't jump he'd stick his cock up my ass." "Did you jump?" asks his girlfriend, "Well, yes," replies the private. "A little bit at first!"

Small People

A man comes home and finds his wife having sex with a midget from the local circus. "I don't believe it!" he cries. "First, it was the ringmaster, then a clown and now a midget!" His wife replies, "Well, at least I'm cutting back!"

• • • • •

A midget with a speech impediment goes to buy a horse from a farmer. The farmer shows the midget the horse in question and the midget asks, "Can I see her muff?" The farmer lifts up the midget so he can examine the horse's mouth. The midget then asks, "Can I see her eerth?" The farmer lifts up the midget so he can look in the horse's ears. The midget then asks, "Can I see her ostwils?" So the farmer lifts up the midget so he can see the horse's nostrils. Then the midget asks, "Can I see her twat?" The farmer—who is now pretty sick and tired of the midget—lifts up the little man and sticks his head up the horse's vagina. After a few seconds he pulls the midget free and puts him down. The midget wipes goo off his face and says, "Pewhaps I can wephrase the wequest: Can I fee her walk about a bit?"

· · · · ·

A woman meets a midget at a party. The woman is eager for a new sexual experience so she ends up taking the midget home with her. "So, what's it going to be like making love to a midget?" asks the woman. The midget replies, "Just take off your clothes, lie back, spread your legs and close your eyes." The woman does so and soon feels something huge pushing into her. The sensation is so fantastic she has a series of incredible orgasms. "Oh, my God!" shouts the woman. "That's the best sex I've ever had!" "Hey," says the midget. "If you thought that was good, just wait till I get the other leg in there!"

· · · · ·

Two midgets go to a bar, pick up a couple of prostitutes and take them to their hotel. Sadly the first midget is unable to get an erection. His depression is enhanced by sounds coming from his friend's room: All night long he hears his friend shouting, "One, two, three... Uuuh! One, two, three… Uuuh…!" In the morning, the second midget asks the first what sort of night he had. "It was so embarrassing," says the first midget. "I just couldn't get a hard-on." The second midget shakes his head. "You think that's embarrassing? I couldn't even get on the bed!"

•••••

A midget is at a singles party. He sidles up to a tall blonde and says, "Hey, what do you say to a little fuck?" She replies, "Hello there, Little Fuck."

Sperm

A masked man bursts into a sperm bank, points a gun at the woman behind the counter and shouts, "Open that fridge behind you." The woman opens the fridge. "Now, take out one of the sperm bottles and drink it," demands the man. The woman takes a deep breath and does so. Just as she finishes gulping down the cold goo, the man takes his mask off. The woman realizes it's her husband. "There," he says. "That wasn't so hard, was it?"

•••••

How do you know if a guy has a high sperm count? His girlfriend has to chew before swallowing!

•••••

I've tried to help childless couples by making anonymous donations of my sperm. However, I've now been told I really should be doing this through a clinic—not just straight through peoples' mailboxes!

• • • • •

One sperm asks another, "How far is it to the ovaries?" The other says, "Relax—we just passed the tonsils!"

Spicing Up the Love Life

A man is speaking to his wife, "I like kinky sex. How about I blow my load in your ear?" "No, you can't!" says his wife. "I might go deaf!" "What d'you mean?" continues the man. "I've been shooting my wads into your mouth for the last twenty years and you're still fucking talking, aren't you?"

• • • • •

A man keeps nagging his wife to have sex in more imaginative positions. He particularly wants to do it doggy style. His wife refuses until, after weeks of pestering, she finally gives in. "Okay," she says. "We'll do it doggy style but I get a blanket to lie on and we're *not* doing it in our street!"

• • • • •

A seven-foot man marries a tiny girl, who's only four feet tall. After the honeymoon a friend asks him how the pair manage to have sex. The man says, "Well, I just sit there, naked, on a chair. She sits on top, and I bob her up and down." "That sounds okay," says the friend. The man replies, "Yeah, it's not so bad. It's a bit like jerking off, only I have somebody to talk to."

• • • • •

A sex therapist is suggesting ways a couple can improve their sex life. "For example," he says. "Why not vary your position? You might try the 'wheelbarrow'—your wife gets on her hands and knees, you lift her legs, penetrate and off you go!" The husband is eager to try this out as soon as they get home. "Well, okay," says the hesitant wife. "But on two conditions: First, if it hurts, you'll stop straight away. And second, you have to promise we won't go past my mother's house!"

•••••

Buck, Tom and their wives decide to spice up their sex lives by swapping partners. Later that night Tom rolls over in bed and says, "Hey, Buck. What d'you suppose our wives are up to?"

•••••

How does a married couple do it doggie style? He sits up and begs while she lies down and plays dead!

•••••

Husband to wife: "Honey, tonight why don't we try changing positions?" Wife: "Okay, you stand by the sink and I'll lie on the sofa!"

•••••

I had two women in my bed the other day. I got home from work and discovered my wife is having a lesbian affair.

•••••

Jane wants to spice up her love life so she buys a pair of crotchless panties. She lies on the bed waiting for her husband to come home. When he opens the bedroom door, she spreads her legs and says, "Hey, want a piece of this?"

"Shit, no!" her horrified husband replies. "Look what it's done to your pants!"

•••••

Suzanne is telling Jane about a new sex game she enjoys playing with her husband. "It's really exciting," she says. "Bill and I sit opposite each other on the floor naked. Then Bill throws grapes at my pussy and I throw doughnuts at his penis. If Bill gets a grape in my vagina, he gets to eat it and if I get a doughnut over his erection, I get to eat that. It's made our love life much more interesting." "Y'know, I'm going to try that with John," says Jane. "D'you think the shop on the corner will be open this late in the evening?" "I'm not sure," replies Suzanne. "But I don't think they sell doughnuts or grapes." "I don't need doughnuts and grapes," replies Jane. "I need a packet of Cheerios and a sack of apples…"

Spiders

Why do black widow spiders kill their mates after sex? To stop the snoring before it starts!

Sports

A Miami player is transferred to San Diego but his first game doesn't get off to a good start. In fact, a substitute comes on and tells him the coach is going to pull him off at half time. "Fantastic," says the player. "At Miami we only got half an orange and a bottle of water."

•••••

A Jew, a Catholic and a Muslim are boasting about their families. The Jewish man says, "I have four sons. One more, and I'll have a basketball team." The Catholic says, "So what? I have ten sons. One more, and I'll have a football team." The Muslim says, "That's nothing. I have seventeen wives. One more, and I'll have a golf course!"

•••••

A Boston Red Sox fan dies and goes to heaven. He's greeted at the Pearly Gates by Saint Peter, who's wearing a New York Yankees scarf. "We don't want your kind in here!" shouts Saint Peter. "Go away!" "But I've been a good man," complains the Red Sox fan. "You have to let me in." "Okay, so what were your last three good deeds?" asks Saint Peter. "Er… I gave $10 to a children's charity," says the fan. "And before that I gave $10 to a cancer charity, and before that I gave $10 to an animal charity." "Hang on," says Saint Peter. "I'll go and ask the boss." Ten minutes later Saint Peter returns with some money. "I had a word with God and he agrees with me. Here's your thirty dollars back. Now fuck off!"

•••••

A racecar driver picks up a girl and takes her to bed. He falls asleep, but wakes up with a start when she smacks his face. "What's the matter?" says the driver. "I thought you liked me?" "I did, till you passed out," replies the girl. "You started to feel my tits in your sleep and said I had perfect headlights. Then you felt my thighs and said I had a smooth finish." "What's wrong with that?" asks the driver. "Nothing," replies the girl. "But then you felt my pussy and said, 'Who the hell left the garage door open?'"

•••••

An old man and his wife are in bed. The old man farts and says, "Seven points." "What in the world are you talking about?" asks his wife. "I'm playing fart football," says the old man. His wife decides to join in. She lets one go and says, "Touchdown! Tie score." The old man farts back and says, "Touchdown! I'm ahead fourteen to seven." His wife squeezes out another one and says, "Touchdown! Tie score." She then strains some more to let out a little squeaker and says, "Field goal! I lead seventeen to fourteen." Not to be outdone, the old man strains as hard as he can but instead of farting, he craps in the bed. His wife looks at him and says, "What in the Lord's name was *that*?" The old man replies, "Halftime—switch sides!"

•••••

At the start of the second half of a football game the men of one team drop their trunks and start masturbating. The coach runs onto the field and yells, "What the hell d'you think you're doing!?" To which the quarterback replies, "You told us to come out here and pull ourselves together!"

•••••

Why does Mike Tyson always have tears in his eyes when he's having sex? Mace!

Stains

A blonde, a brunette and a redhead are riding in an elevator. The redhead notices a spot on the elevator wall and says, "That looks like a cum stain." The brunette leans over and smells the stain. "It sure smells like a cum stain," she says. The blonde leans over and tastes the spot. "It *is* a cum stain," she says. "But it's nobody from this building!"

•••••

A little girl and her mother are walking through the park when they see two teenagers having sex on a bench. The little girl says, "Mommy, what are they doing?" Mother replies, "Um, they're making cakes." The next day they're at a zoo and the little girl sees two monkeys having sex. Again, she asks her mother what they're doing. Mother replies with the same response—making cakes. The next day the girl says to her mother, "Mommy, I know you and Daddy were making cakes in the living room last night." Mother says, "Oh yes? And how would you know that?" The girl replies, "Because I licked the icing off the sofa!"

•••••

Did you hear about the man who named his dog "Stain"? The police arrested him for wandering the streets yelling, "Come, Stain! Come, Stain!"

Stranded

A married couple have been stranded on a deserted island for many years. One day another man, Joe, washes up on shore. Joe and the wife become attracted to each other, but realize they must be creative if they're to engage in any hanky-panky. The husband is also pleased that Joe has arrived on the island. "Great," he says. "Now we'll be able to have three people doing eight-hour shifts in the watchtower." Joe volunteers to do the first shift and climbs up the tower. The couple on the ground start making a fire to cook supper. Joe yells down, "Hey, no screwing!" The couple yell back, "We're not screwing!" A few minutes later the couple start repairing a fishing net. Joe yells down, "Hey, no screwing!" Again, they yell back, "We're not screwing!" Later, the couple are putting palm leaves on the roof of their hut. Again, Joe yells down, "Hey, I said no screwing!" They yell back, "We're not screwing!" Eventually the shift is over. Joe climbs down the tower and the husband takes over. The husband climbs the tower. At the top he looks down and says, "Well, I'll be... He was right. From up here it *does* look like they're screwing!"

Super Heroes

Batman meets Superman on the street one day. He notices that Superman's cape is torn and he's covered with bruises. Batman asks what happened and Superman explains, "I was flying over the city when I spotted Cat Woman on a roof, sunbathing in the nude with her legs spread. I couldn't help myself, so I whipped out my dick, flew down there and landed right between her thighs." "Was she surprised?" asks Batman. "Sure," Superman replies. "But not half as surprised as the Invisible Man!"

Swearing

How do you make a group of old ladies shout "fuck"? Say "bingo!"

•••••

Two brothers are sent home from school for swearing. Their father gives them a beating and sends them straight to bed. In the morning he asks the boys what they'd like for breakfast. The first boy says, "I'll have fucking cereal." His father gives the boy a thrashing and sends him back to his room. He then turns to the second boy and asks him what he'd like for his breakfast. "I'm not sure," says the boy. "But I tell you one thing—it's not going to be fucking cereal!"

•••••

A man walks into a bank. After waiting twenty minutes in line, he goes to the customer services desk. "Hey, fuck face!" he says. "I got this fucking check to deposit and I'll be fucked if I'm going to wait in that fucking line any more!" "Please, sir," says the woman, "Try and tone down your language." "Never mind my fucking language!" shouts the man. "This fucking check isn't doing me any good sitting in my fucking shitting pocket!" "Sir," says the woman. "Please calm down, or I'll have to ask you to leave." "Fuck you, ass breath!" shouts the man. "I don't have to take this fucking shit from you! Get the fucking manager out here!" The manager is called over and asks what the commotion is about. "I'll tell you what it's about," says the man. "It's about me trying to deposit this fucking check for fifteen million dollars! That's what it's about!"

"Fifteen million dollars?" says the manager, looking at the woman. "And this fucking bitch won't help you?"

Tarzan

Tarzan meets Jane for the first time and they get chatting in his tree house. "Hope you don't mind me asking," says Jane. "But what does a man like you do for sex around here?" Tarzan points at a hole in the tree and says, "There—hole very good." Jane strips off and lies on the floor with her legs open. "I think I can do better than that," she says. "Try putting it in here." Tarzan peers at her crotch, then takes off his loincloth and kicks Jane in the crotch. "Argh!" she cries. "What did you do that for?" Tarzan replies, "Checking for bees!"

Tattoos

A woman goes to a tattooist to have a picture of Lennox Lewis tattooed on her right inner thigh, and a picture of Mike Tyson tattooed on her left inner thigh. However, when the tattooist is finished, the woman is appalled at the quality of his handiwork. She goes into the manager's office, sits on his desk and opens her legs. "Excuse me," she says. "But do you really think that looks like Lennox Lewis, or that looks like Mike Tyson?" "No," replies the manager, "But that one in the middle definitely looks like Don King!"

• • • • •

John has his new bride's name, Wendy, tattooed on his penis. Normally, only the first and last letters, "W" and "Y," are visible, and it's only when he's erect that the whole name can be seen. John and Wendy go on honeymoon to Jamaica and one evening John finds himself standing at a hotel urinal next to one of the locals. To his surprise he notices that the man also has the letters "W" and "Y" tattooed on his penis. "Excuse me," he says, "but I couldn't help noticing your tattoo. Do you have a girlfriend named Wendy?" "No," says the man. "I work for the Tourist board. My tattoo says, 'Welcome to Jamaica, my friend, have a nice day.'"

The Ways They Do It...

Accountants love examining figures.

Actors do it on cue.

Ambulance drivers come quicker.

Assembly line workers do it over and over.

Astronomers do it with Uranus.

Australians like to do it down under.

Bailiffs always come to order.

Bakers knead it daily.

Bankers do it with interest—but will give you a penalty for early withdrawal.

Bartenders do it on the rocks.

Beer drinkers like a good bit of head.

Bookkeepers use the double entry method.

Bosses get someone else to do it for them.

Bus drivers come early, but should pull out on time.

Chemists like to experiment.

Chess players are quick to mate.

Computer game players just can't stop.

Computer operators do the best they can with their software.

Construction workers will lay a better foundation.

Consultants enjoy telling other people how to do it.

Cowboys do it with anything horny.

Crane operators do it with swinging balls.

Cyclists do it at ten different speeds.

Deer hunters will do anything for a quick buck.

Dental hygienists do it till it hurts.

Dentists do it in your mouth.

Detectives do it under cover.

Divers do it deep down.

Doctors do it with patience.

Drummers do it in 4/4 time.

Electricians are always checking out your shorts.

Engineers will charge you by the hour.

Estate agents do it in much sought-after areas.

Executives do it with a large staff.

Farmers spread it around.

Firemen are always in heat.

Fishermen do it with their rods and their tackle.

Flight attendants do it in the air.

Garbage men only come once a week.

Gardeners do it with 50-foot hoses.

Gas station attendants can pump away all day.

Geologists are great explorers.

Golfers can do eighteen holes.

Hairdressers are known for giving the best blow jobs.

Handymen enjoy a good screw.

Hunters do it with a bang.

Interior decorators do it all over the house.

Inventors can always find a way.

Janitors always clean up afterward.

Joggers do it on the run.

Lawyers do it in their briefs.

Librarians do it quietly.

Locksmiths can get into anything.

Motorcyclists always like something powerful and hot between their legs.

Painters do it with longer strokes.

Photographers do it with a flash.

Pilots stay up longer.

Plumbers do it under the sink.

Proctologists do it in the end.

Publishers do it by the book.

Racers like to come in first.

Real estate people know all the prime spots.

Recyclers do it again and again.

Retailers like to move their merchandise.

Roofers do it on top.

Salesmen have a way with their tongues.

Secretaries do it from 9 to 5.

Skydivers are good till the last drop.

Soccer players do it with leather balls.

Sports announcers do it followed by an instant replay.

Tailors make it fit comfortably.

Taxi drivers do it all over town.

Taxidermists will mount anything.

Telephone company employees let their fingers do the walking.

Tennis players do it with fuzzy green balls.

Truck drivers have the biggest dipsticks and carry the biggest loads.

Typists do it in triplicate.

Welders have the hottest rods.

Writers have novel ways.

Zoologists do it with animal instinct.

Toilets and Related Problems

A man is on an airplane. He has to take a shit really badly, but all the men's toilets are occupied. The flight attendant tells him he can use the women's restroom. "But," she warns, "don't touch any button except for the flush." After taking a dump, the man notices three buttons next to the flush button. One is marked "WW," one is marked "PP," and the third is marked "ATR." Curious, he decides to try them out. He pushes the "WW" button and warm water cleans his asshole and cock. He pushes the "PP" button and a powder puff rubs powder on his ass and dick. "Wow!" thinks the man. "This is great!" Then he pushes the "ATR" button... The next thing he knows, he's waking up in a hospital. The flight attendant is standing by his bedside. "What happened?" he asks. "You touched the 'ATR' button, didn't you?" asks the flight attendant. "I did," says the man. "Well," replies the flight attendant. "'ATR' stands for 'Automatic Tampon Remover' and your dick is in that jar on that table!"

•••••

What do a vagina and a warm toilet seat have in common? They're both nice but you always wonder who was there before you.

•••••

A man comes back from a safari and tells his friend about a narrow escape. "I was walking by a water hole when a lion jumped out at me, so I ran for the tents," says the man. "It almost caught up with me but it slipped and I managed to jump over a log. The lion jumped over the log as well, but then it slipped again and fell over. By this time I was almost at the camp. I could see the safari guide with his gun so I shouted for help. The guide took aim but he couldn't fire because the lion was only a few feet behind me. It leapt up at me, then it slipped again and I had just enough time to duck into a tent before the guide shot it." "Jesus!" his friend exclaims. "If that had happened to me, I'd have crapped myself." "I did," replies the man. "Why do you think the lion kept slipping?"

•••••

"Knock, knock!" "Who's there?" "I Dunop." "I Dunop who?"

•••••

A man goes to his doctor suffering from constipation. The doctor prescribes a powerful laxative but asks the man some questions so he can calculate the right dosage. "How long will it take you to get home from here?" asks the doctor. "Ten minutes," the man replies. The doctor pours a dose of laxative into a glass. "And how long will it take you to get from the front door of your house to your bathroom?" asks the doctor. "I suppose about twenty seconds," says the man. The doctor adds a small amount of laxative to the glass. "And how long will it take you to drop your pants and sit on the toilet?" asks the doctor. "I'd say five seconds," the man replies. The doctor adds a tiny amount of laxative to the glass and gives it to the man. "Take that, drink it all down and go straight home," says the doctor. The next day the doctor calls the man to see how he's feeling. "Not so good," replies the man. "Didn't the laxative work?" asks the doctor. "Oh yeah, it worked fine," the man replies. "But it was seven seconds early!"

•••••

A man goes to the doctor with a bowel problem and is prescribed a course of suppositories. The doctor inserts the first suppository, then sends the man home to continue the course of treatment: one suppository every six hours. The time comes for the next suppository and the man tries to stick the lozenge up his anus himself. It's very tricky, so the man calls in his wife to help. She grabs hold of his arm to keep him steady and pushes the pill inside her husband using an index finger. Suddenly the man lets out a scream. "What's the matter?" asks his wife. "Did I push too hard?" "No," her husband replies. "I've just realized something—when the doctor did it, he had both his hands on my shoulders!"

•••••

A man is driving through the middle of nowhere when suddenly he's desperate to get to the toilet for a good sit-down. So he pulls over at a rundown roadside store and dashes into their bathroom. He does his business but then realizes there's no toilet paper. Then he sees a sign on the wall: "Revolutionary new bathroom hygiene system. Simply wipe yourself with your fingers and then place them in the hole below." So he wipes his ass with his fingers then sticks them in the washing hole. It works! Someone whacks his fingers between two bricks and he recoils and shoves them straight into his mouth.

•••••

A man sitting in a public toilet discovers there's no toilet paper. He calls into the next booth, "Do you have any tissue paper in there?" "No," comes the reply. "Do you have any newspaper?" asks the man. "Sorry!" is the reply. "Okay," says the man. "So could you give me two fives for a ten?"

•••••

A nurse walks into a hospital waiting room and smells crap. "Who the hell shit in their pants?" she demands. No one answers and so, determined to find the guilty party, she walks down the line of patients and smells them. Finally, she discovers the culprit: an old drunk in the corner. "Hey!" she says. "How come you didn't answer when I asked who shit their pants?" "Oh," replies the drunk. "I thought you meant *today*!"

•••••

A teenager is giving his grandpa a lift. He pulls out into the heavy traffic so fast he burns rubber and the tires start smoking. "Phewee!" says the young driver. "Can you smell that shit?" Terrified, Grandpa replies, "Sure I can smell it! I'm sitting in it!"

•••••

Bob goes into a public toilet and sees a man with no arms standing next to the urinal. He takes a pee and is about to leave when the man asks, "Can you help me unzip my zipper?" "Er, sure," replies Bob, undoing the zipper. Then the man asks, "Can you take it out for me?" Bob says, "Um, okay." He pulls out the man's penis and sees that it's covered in all kinds of moldy red bumps, oozing yellow holes and brown scabs. "Could you point it for me?" asks the man. "Sure thing," says Bob, holding it steady. "Could you put it back in?" asks the man when he's finished. "Will do," says Bob, shaking it dry and putting it back in his pants. "Thanks," says the man. "I really appreciate that." "No problem," says Bob. "But I've got to ask you—what the hell is wrong with your penis?" The guy pulls his arms out of his shirt and says, "Damned if I know, but I sure ain't touching it!"

•••••

Did you hear about the constipated accountant? He couldn't budget!

Did you hear about the constipated composer? He got stuck on his last movement!

Did you hear about the constipated mathematician? He worked it out with a pencil!

Four out of five people say they suffer from diarrhea— so does that mean that one out of the five actually enjoys it?

Go with the flow—be a bed wetter.

If diarrhea only runs down one leg, is it called monorrhea?

•••••

Julian is standing at a public urinal when a huge man bursts in, waving an enormous dick. The man whacks his dick against a mirror, and the mirror shatters. He swings it against a sink, and the sink smashes. Then he thumps the condom machine with his dick, and the machine's wrenched off the wall. Finally, the guy comes over to Julian, panting like a bull. "Now," says the man. "I am going to fuck you up the ass!" "Oh, thank God," says Julian. "I thought you were going to hit me with it!"

•••••

Life is a little like being a pubic hair on the side of a toilet bowl. Eventually you get pissed off!

•••••

Three old men are comparing ailments. "I've got a problem," says one, "Every morning at seven o'clock I get up and I try to urinate, but I can never manage it." The second old man says, "You think you've got a problem? Every morning at eight I get up and try to move my bowels, but it never works." The third old man speaks up, "Every morning at seven I urinate and every morning at eight I defecate." "So you've got no problems then?" asks the first man. "Sure I do," replies the third man. "I don't wake up till nine!"

•••••

What's the difference between a girl and a toilet? A toilet doesn't want to cuddle after you drop a load in it!

Tramps and Vagrancy

A tramp finds a $5 bill and decides to spend it on a bottle of cheap sherry. He downs the whole bottle in one go and collapses unconscious up an alley. A passing gay man happens to find him lying passed out and makes the most of the opportunity. He pulls down the tramp's pants and screws him. When he's finished, he presses a $5 bill into the tramp's hand as a thank-you and leaves. The tramp wakes up the next day, finds the bill and spends it on another bottle of sherry. Exactly the same thing happens again. The gay guy finds the tramp unconscious in the alley, screws him, and leaves him with another fiver. After four bottles of sherry the tramp staggers into the liquor store with his latest fiver. "You again," says the shopkeeper. "I suppose you want more sherry?" The tramp looks at the shelves of booze. "I don't know," he replies. "I ought to try something else—sherry really makes my ass hurt!"

•••••

A tramp walks into a bar and asks for a cocktail swizzle stick. The bartender gives him one and the tramp hurries outside. Ten minutes later he comes back in and asks for another one. The bartender gives him a second swizzle stick and the tramp hurries out again. Fifteen minutes later the tramp returns and the bartender hands over a third swizzle stick. "Could I have a straw instead?" asks the tramp. "Someone's been sick on the pavement, but now all the lumpy bits have gone!"

•••••

A man walks into a bar and sits next to an old drunk. The man smells a foul odor, turns to the drunk and says, "Christ! Did you crap your pants, you old bastard?" "Yup," replies the tramp. "Then why don't you go to the bathroom?" asks the man. The drunk replies, "'Cause I ain't finished yet!"

•••••

A tramp walks into a nightclub and says, "For free drinks I'll get on your stage tonight and fart 'Dixie.'" The club owner agrees and that night the tramp shuffles onstage and drops his pants. He then proceeds to take a big shit on the floor. "What the hell!" shouts the club owner. "You said you were going to fart 'Dixie'!" "I am," says the tramp. "I'm just clearing my throat first!"

•••••

What's the best part of having a homeless girlfriend? You can drop her off wherever you like!

Twins

A musician starts talking to a couple of girls in a bar, who turn out to be Siamese twins. The girls wind up back at the man's apartment and he eventually talks them into bed. He makes love to one girl, then starts to work on the other. He's worried that the first girl might get bored, so he asks her if she wants the TV turned on. The girl declines, but asks to play a trombone she's seen lying on the floor. She turns out to be a great trombone player and she serenades the man as he screws her sister. A few weeks later, the girls are walking past the man's apartment building. One of the girls says, "Hey, let's stop by and see that guy." The other girl says, "Gee… do you think he'd remember us?"

Uncontrollable Erections

An old man wakes up in the middle of the night and finds that his pecker is as hard as a rock for the first time in years. He wakes his wife and shows her his erection. "Look at that!" he exclaims happily. "What do you think we ought to do with it?" "Well," his wife replies. "Seeing as you've got all the wrinkles out, now might be a good time to wash it!"

•••••

Steve has a crush on a girl at work. He's dying to ask her out on a date, but every time he sees her he gets a huge uncontrollable erection. One day he summons up the nerve to call her and they arrange to go on a date. To prepare for their evening Steve ties his penis to his leg so he won't embarrass himself. He arrives at the girl's house and rings on her doorbell. Unfortunately she answers the door in her underwear and Steve kicks her in the face…

Vasectomy

A newly married couple are arguing about how many children to have. The wife says she wants three, while the husband says two will be enough. The argument gets extremely heated and eventually the husband says, "After our second child, I'll just have a vasectomy." His wife replies, "Well then, I hope you'll love the third one as if it were one of your own!"

•••••

A redneck goes to his doctor to get a vasectomy but is horrified when he finds out how much they cost. "I could do you a cheap one," says the doctor. "But it's painful." "I can take it," the redneck replies, so the doctor hands him a large firecracker. "Take this home," he says. "Light it and hold it in your hand while counting to ten." "How's that going to give me a vasectomy?" asks the redneck. "You'll find out," says the doctor. The redneck takes the firecracker home, lights it and holds it in his right hand while he counts to ten. When he gets to five he tucks the firecracker between his legs and holds up his left hand: "…six, seven, eight…"

•••••

What's the definition of macho? Jogging home after a vasectomy!

Vegetables

One day a cucumber, a pickle and a penis are having a conversation. The pickle says, "My life really sucks—whenever I get big, fat and juicy they sprinkle seasonings over me and stick me in a jar!" The cucumber says, "You think that's bad? Whenever I get big, fat and juicy, they slice me up and they put me in a salad!" Then the penis pipes up, "You think that's tough? Whenever I get big, fat and juicy, they throw a plastic bag over my head, shove me in a wet, dark, smelly room and force me to do push-ups until I throw up!"

Viagra

A lady walks into a pharmacy and asks, "Do you have Viagra?" "Yes," replies the pharmacist. "Does it work?" inquires the lady. "Certainly," says the pharmacist. "Can you get it over the counter?" the lady continues. "Only if I take six!" replies the pharmacist.

• • • • •

A little old man goes into a pharmacy to buy some Viagra. "Can I have twelve tablets, please," he asks. "And could you cut them into quarters for me?" The clerk says, "A quarter of a tablet won't be enough to give you a full erection, you know." "That's alright," says the old man. "I'm 96 years old—I don't have much use for an erection. I just want to make it stick out far enough so I don't piss on my shoes!"

• • • • •

A man falls asleep on a beach and gets severe sunburn. Rushed to hospital by his wife, the doctor rubs lotion over him and prescribes Viagra. "Viagra!" exclaims the wife. "What good is Viagra in his condition?" The doctor replies, "It'll help keep the sheets off him!"

• • • • •

A man gets a prescription for Viagra. He goes home but finds his wife is out shopping so he calls her on the phone,

"I've just taken some Viagra," he says. "Get home as soon as you can!" His wife climbs into her car and starts making her way home, but gets stuck in traffic. An hour passes and then another, and the man becomes frustrated. He calls his doctor for advice. The doctor suggests, "It's a shame to waste the erection. Do you have a housekeeper? Maybe you can use it on her instead?" The man replies, "But I don't *need* Viagra with the housekeeper..."

• • • • •

A man goes to his doctor asking for a Viagra prescription. "But I'll need an extra big dose," he explains. "I've got two young nymphomaniacs spending a whole week at my place." Later that week, the man comes back asking for painkillers. "Why?" the doctor asks. "Has your penis been damaged?" "No," replies the man, "It's for my wrist—the bitches never showed up!"

• • • • •

A woman asks her husband if he'd like some breakfast. "Bacon and eggs... perhaps a slice of toast? Maybe some grapefruit, and a cup of coffee?" The husband declines. "It's this Viagra, it's really taken the edge off my appetite," he explains. At noon, she asks if he would like some lunch. "A bowl of soup perhaps... maybe a cheese sandwich? Or how about a bowl of chili and a glass of milk?" Again the husband declines. "No, thanks—it's this Viagra," he says, "I really don't feel hungry at all." At dinnertime, she asks if he wants anything to eat, "How about a pizza or a stir-fry? That'll only take a couple of minutes..." Once more, the husband declines. "No, thanks—it's this Viagra. I really don't feel like eating anything." "Okay, I get it," says his wife, "But would you mind getting the hell off me for a minute? I am fucking STARVING!"

• • • • •

An old man walks into a pharmacy and asks for a bottle of Viagra. "Do you have a prescription?" asks the pharmacist. "No," replies the old man. "But here's a picture of my wife…"

• • • • •

Did you hear about the 15-year-old boy who ate a bottle of Viagra? He was rushed to hospital with third degree friction burns.

• • • • •

Did you hear about the lesbian who took too much Viagra? She couldn't get her tongue back into her head for a week!

• • • • •

Following the approval of Viagra by the FDA, the first shipment arrived yesterday at JFK airport; however, it was hijacked on the way to the warehouse. The FBI have warned the public to be on the lookout for a gang of hardened criminals.

• • • • •

Have you heard about the Viagra computer virus? It turns your 3.5 inch floppy into a hard disk.

• • • • •

In pharmacology, all drugs have a generic name: Tylenol is acetaminophen, Advil is ibuprofen, and so on. The FDA has been looking for a generic name for Viagra: They announced today that they have settled on mycoxafloppin.

•••••

Mix Viagra and Prozac and you have a guy who is ready to go, but doesn't really care where.

•••••

Since the release of Viagra, exotic dancers now claim they're receiving a lot more standing ovations.

•••••

They've started giving Viagra to old men in nursing homes... It keeps them from rolling out of bed!

•••••

Viagra—the gift that keeps on coming.

Virginity

A bride-to-be confesses to a friend that she's not a virgin. "No problem," says the friend. "Go out and buy a piece of liver. Put it inside you before you get into bed and you'll feel nice and tight. He'll never know the difference." The bride does as suggested and on the wedding night she and her new husband screw like crazy. They fuck on the floor, on the kitchen table, in the bathroom and in the bed. They have a fantastic time, but the next morning the bride is horrified to discover that her new husband has vanished. She finds a note on the bedside table. It reads: "I love you very much, but I have realized we can't go on like this. We can never have a life together. Farewell. P.S. Your vagina is in the sink."

•••••

A couple are on their honeymoon. "Please be gentle," says the bride. "I'm still a virgin." "What!" her husband exclaims. "How can you be a virgin? You've already been married three times!" "Yes," replies the bride. "But my first husband was a gynecologist, and all he did was look at it. My second husband was a psychiatrist, and all he did was talk about it. And my third husband was a stamp collector, and all he did was... Aaah, gee, I do miss him!"

•••••

A man and woman are lying in bed after making love. The man mutters to himself saying, "Man, oh man, I finally did it! I'm not a virgin anymore." The woman overhears this and says, "Are you saying you just lost your virginity to me?" "Yes," says the man. "When I was young I vowed that I would wait to give my virginity to the woman I love." Astounded, the woman replies, "So, you must really love me?" "Naah," says the guy. "I just got sick of waiting!"

•••••

A man in a hotel bar sees a beautiful woman sitting alone at a table. He goes over to pick her up. After talking to her for a while he invites her back to his room. "I can't," says the woman. "I'm saving my virginity until I meet a man who I can truly love." "That must be hard," says the man. "Oh, I don't mind so much," says the woman. "It's my husband who's really pissed off!"

•••••

A man out on the golf course takes a high-speed ball right in the crotch. Writhing in agony, he's taken to a doctor.

"Can you fix it, Doc?" he asks. "I'm getting married on Friday. Can you give me something to get me through the ceremony?" The doctor tells him not to worry. He prescribes some painkillers, then makes a splint out of four tongue depressors, which he wires together to form a protective cage. Later that week the man gets married and he and his bride end up in the honeymoon suite. "You do realize I'm a virgin," says the girl. She opens her dress and exposes her breasts. "You'll be the first—no man has ever touched these before." "You think that's something?" replies the man, taking off his pants, "Look at this—it's still in its crate!"

• • • • •

A young woman comes home from her first semester in college. She confesses to her mother that she lost her virginity the previous weekend. "It was bound to happen sooner or later," says her mother. "I just hope it was a romantic and pleasurable experience." "Yes and no," the girl replies. "The first eight guys felt great, but after that my pussy got really sore!"

• • • • •

An old woman dies a virgin and requests the following inscription on her headstone: "Born a virgin, lived a virgin, died a virgin." The undertaker decides to economize, so he inscribes, "Returned, unopened."

• • • • •

How can you tell if a redneck girl is a virgin? She can outrun her brothers!

• • • • •

What did the Tennessee girl say just after she lost her virginity? "Get off me, Daddy. Ya'll squashin' ma" cigarettes!"

What's the Difference...?

What's the difference between a clever midget and a venereal disease? One's a cunning runt.

What's the difference between erotic and kinky? Erotic is using a feather—kinky is using the whole chicken.

What's the difference between snowmen and snow women? Snowballs.

What's the difference between "light" and "hard"? You can sleep with the light on.

What's the difference between a bitch and a whore? A whore sleeps with everybody at the party; a bitch sleeps with everybody at the party except you.

What's the difference between a door and a woman? When you lubricate it, the door stops squealing.

What's the difference between a poodle humping your leg and a pit bull humping your leg? You let the pit bull finish.

What's the difference between a cheese cracker and a lesbian? One's a snack cracker, the other a crack snacker!

What's the difference between a whorehouse and a circus? One is a cunning array of stunts.

What's the difference between a wife and a prostitute? With a prostitute you get what you paid for!

What's the difference between acne and a priest? Acne usually comes on a boy's face *after* he turns 14.

What's the difference between tear gas, an onion, and a fourteen-inch dick? Nothing, they all make your eyes water.

What's the difference between doing a 69 and driving through a speed trap? With a 69, you can see the prick coming.

What's the difference between love, true love and showing off? Spitting, swallowing and gargling.

What's the difference between your wife and your job? After five years your job will still suck.

Wishes

A man finds a magic lamp and rubs it. A genie appears and grants him one wish. The man is embarrassed so he leans down and whispers it in the genie's ear. The genie looks surprised but shrugs his shoulders and says, "Okay, if that's what you want. Your wish will be granted at midnight." That night the clock strikes twelve and the man hears knocking on his front door. He opens it and finds two slaughterhouse men standing outside holding a rope. "Hi," says one. "Are you the guy who wants to be hung like a donkey?"

• • • • •

A man finds a magic lamp, rubs it and releases a genie. "What is your wish?" asks the genie. "Well, I'm a real sex maniac," says the man. "So I wish that I'm always hard and I get more ass than any man who ever lived." So the genie turns him into a toilet bowl.

• • • • •

A man walks into a bar with a giant cork shoved up his backside. The bartender asks him how it happened. "I was walking along the beach," says the man, "and I found a lamp. So I picked it up to brush it off, and a genie popped out. The genie me told me he'd grant me a wish, so I said, 'Wow! No shit!'"

• • • • •

A man with a fifty-inch penis is desperate to get it shortened, so he visits a witch doctor to see if he can help. "Go into the forest," says the witch doctor. "There, by a magic pool, you will find a magic frog. Ask the frog to marry you and each time it refuses, your dick will shrink by ten inches." The man is skeptical, but goes into the forest and sure enough, finds a magic frog sitting by a magic pool. "Magic frog!" shouts the man. "Please marry me!" "No!" croaks the frog. The man looks down and sees that his dick is now only forty inches long. It's still too long, however, so he calls out again, "Please marry me, magic frog!" "No!" shouts back the frog. "I told you once!" The man looks down and finds his dick is now only thirty inches long. The man wants to take off another ten inches, so he shouts, "Oh go on, Mister Frog! Please marry me!" The frog is really irritated and shouts back, "No, no! And for the last time… NO!"

• • • • •

A woman buys a mirror at an antique shop, and hangs it on her bathroom door. One evening she playfully says, "Mirror, mirror on my door, make my bust size 44." There's a brilliant flash of light, and her boobs grow to enormous proportions. She runs to tell her husband what's happened. He rushes into the bathroom and says, "Mirror, mirror, on the door, make my dick touch the floor!" There's a brilliant flash of light and both his legs fall off!

•••••

An American, an Englishman and a Polish man are trapped on top of a cliff. The only way down is to jump. Suddenly, the American spots an old lamp. He picks it up and rubs it. Pop! Out comes a genie. "I cannot make you fly," says the genie. "But choose something soft and I will ensure that when you leap from the cliff, you will land on it." The American jumps off the edge of the cliff, shouts out, "Pillows!" and lands safely on a huge pile of pillows. The Englishman takes a running jump, shouts out, "Feathers!" and lands safely on a huge heap of feathers. The Polish guy takes a running jump, trips up and falls over the edge, shouting, "Shit!"

•••••

An old lady is polishing a lamp when a genie suddenly appears and offers her three wishes. "I'd like to be young and beautiful again," says the old lady. "I'd like this cottage to be a fine mansion, and I'd like my cat, Sparky, to be a handsome prince." The genie grants these wishes and the old lady, the cottage and Sparky are all transformed. The beautiful young woman swoons into the handsome prince's arms and he gently whispers in her ear, "Hey, lady. I bet you wish you hadn't paid that vet to cut my balls off."

•••••

Mister Bear and Mister Rabbit are enemies who live in the same forest. One day they come across a magic frog who tells them it will give them three wishes each. Mister Bear wishes that all the other bears in the forest turn into females. Mister Rabbit wishes for a crash helmet. Mister Bear wishes that he has unlimited sexual stamina. Mister Rabbit wishes for a motorcycle. Mister Bear makes his final wish—that he is irresistible to all female bears. The magic frog replies that it has been done. "Okay," says Mister Bear to Mister Rabbit. "You wasted your other two wishes, what are you going to waste your last wish on?" Mister Rabbit puts on the helmet, climbs on the bike, revs the engine, then tears off down the road. Over his shoulder he shouts, "I wish Mister Bear was gay!"

Women

How can you make a woman scream for an hour after sex? Wipe your cock on the curtains.

How do you get a woman off during sex? Push her!

How is a woman like a condom? Both spend more time in your wallet than on your dick.

What two things in the air can make a woman pregnant? Her feet!

Why are hangovers better than women? Hangovers will go away.

Why do women rub their eyes when they wake up? Because they don't have balls to scratch!

Why don't women blink during foreplay? They don't have time.

Why don't women have brains? Because they don't have penises to keep them in!

Why is a good woman like a bar? Liquor in the front, poker in the rear!

Work and Workmen

A construction worker on the fifth floor of a building needs a drill. He gestures to another worker on the ground and, once he's got his attention, he uses sign language to tell him what he wants sent up. First, he points to his eye for "I." Then he points to his knee for "need." And then he mimes using a drill. The worker on the ground gives the thumbs-up, then takes out his dick and starts to masturbate. The other worker can't believe his eyes. He gets into the elevator and goes down to see what's going on. He goes over to the masturbating worker and asks, "What the hell are you doing? I wanted you to get a drill!" "Yeah," the other worker replies. "And I'm telling you, 'I'm coming'!"

• • • • •

A little boy spends the afternoon watching some builders at work on a neighbor's house. When he goes inside his mother asks him what he's been doing. "Learning about building," he replies. "And what did you learn?" she asks. "Well," the boy replies. "First, you put the goddamn door up. Then the son of a bitch doesn't fit, so you have to take the cocksucker down. Then you have to shave a cunt's hair off each side and put the motherfucker back up." "Good God!" his mother exclaims. "Just wait till your father gets home!" When his father returns, he hears the whole story and goes to the little boy's bedroom. "That was appalling language to use in front of your mother!" he says. "You've got to be punished. Go and get me a switch!" "What?" the little boy replies. "Fuck you—that's the electrician's job!"

•••••

A railway worker is lying on the ground in a train station, clutching his stomach and rolling around in pain. "Are you all right?" asks a passenger. "Yeah," says the worker. "But I'm busting for a shit and I don't start work for another fifteen minutes!"

•••••

Harry sees a want ad for a "pussy shaver." He calls up the employment agency and discovers that he'll be required to shave the bikini lines of supermodels at photo shoots in the world's most glamorous locations. Moreover, the job pays $40,000 a year. "Do you think you'd be up to it?" asks the man at the agency. "Sure," says Harry. "Where do I go for the interview?" The man says, "Can you be at 12th Street by eleven o'clock on Monday?" "Yes," replies Harry. "But the ad said the job was based on 1st Street." "It is," replies the man. "But 12th Street is where the line for the interview starts!"

•••••

How can you tell when an auto mechanic just had sex? One of his fingers is clean!

•••••

Three men are talking in a bar. "I think my wife is having an affair with an electrician," says one. "I found a pair of pliers under our bed and they certainly aren't mine." "I think my wife is having an affair with a welder," says the second. "I found a blow-torch under our bed and it sure isn't mine." "I think my wife is having an affair with a horse," says the third. "When I got home yesterday there were two jockeys in the closet!"

•••••

What's the worst thing about the increase in unemployment? It's harder to fuck your girlfriend when her husband's at home!

X-Ray Glasses

A man goes into a shop and sees a pair of x-ray glasses for sale. "What do they do?" he asks. "They let you see everyone in the nude," says the shopkeeper. The man tries on the glasses and immediately everyone he looks at is in the nude. The shopkeeper is nude, his assistant is nude, even a passerby looking in the window is nude. The man buys the glasses and goes out into the street to look at everyone in the nude. After a while he decides to sneak home and surprise his wife. He gets back, creeps in the living room and finds his wife and his neighbor nude on the couch. "Surprise!" he shouts, coming into the room. "What do you think of my new glasses?" He takes them off, but sees that his wife and neighbor are still naked. "Damn!" he says. "I only had them an hour and they're broken already!"

Yo' Momma Insults

Yo' momma's so fat, her ass has it's own congressman.

Yo' momma's so fat, her belly button doesn't have lint, it has sweaters.

Yo' momma's so fat, her belt size is the equator.

Yo' momma's so fat, her chairs have seat belts.

Yo' momma's so fat, the last time she went to Sea World the killer whale got a hard-on.

Yo' momma's so fat, when I climbed on top of her I burned my ass on the light bulb.

Yo' momma's so fat, when I have sex with her I have to slap her ass and ride the wave in.

Yo' momma's so fat, when I tried to fuck her I didn't know if I was hitting the hole or a roll.

Yo' momma's so fat… but I fucked her anyway.

Yo' momma's a carpenter's dream, she's flat as a board and never been screwed.

Yo' momma's got a party in her mouth tonight, and everybody's cummin."

Yo' momma's like a bottle of ketchup—she gets turned around, banged and then she comes out slow.

Yo' momma's like a bowling ball—she gets three fingers, thrown in the gutter, and comes back for more.

Yo' momma's like a doorknob—everyone gets a turn!

Yo' momma's like a "Happy Meal"—small, cheap and greasy!

Yo' momma's like a hardware store—five cents a screw.

Yo' momma's like a pie—everybody gets a piece.

Yo' momma's like a racing car—she burns fifty rubbers a day.

Yo' momma's like a refrigerator—everyone sticks their meat in her.

Yo' momma's like a shotgun—one cock and she'll blow.

Yo' momma's like a television—even a two-year-old could turn her on!

Yo' momma's like a toilet—fat, white and smells like crap.

Yo' momma's like a vacuum cleaner—she sucks, blows and gets laid in the closet.

Yo' momma's like a video game—three men for a quarter.

Yo' momma's like lettuce—25 cents per head.

Yo' momma's like pizza—thirty minutes or it's free!

Yo' momma's like the village bicycle—everybody gets a ride.

Yo' momma's so fat, her diaphragms come in a Domino's pizza box.

Yo' momma's so fat, if you want to have sex with her, you roll her ass in flour and look for the wet spot.

Yo' momma's so fat, when I get on top of her my ears pop.

Yo' momma's so fat, when we were having sex I rolled over nine times and I was still on her.

Yo' momma's so loose, she jerks herself with the fat end of a baseball bat.

Yo' momma's so nasty, I called her for phone sex and she gave me an ear infection.

Yo' momma's so nasty, she has to put ice down her pants to keep the crabs fresh!

Yo' momma's so old, she remembers turning tricks for a nickel.

Yo' momma's so slutty, she could suck a golf ball through six feet of garden hose.

Yo' momma's so slutty, she could suck the chrome off a trailer hitch ball!

Yo' momma's so ugly, she's a living example of why you shouldn't do it with family.

You Know You're Having a Bad Day When...

You bite into a hot dog and find veins.

You dream you were eating a big chocolate pudding, then wake up and find a spoon wedged up your wife's ass.

You take a sip from a bloody mary and find a pubic hair.

You wake up in the morning with a lump in your throat and a string hanging out of your mouth.

Your wife meets you at the door, nude. But she's the one coming in...

•••••

Bad: You find a porn movie in your son's room.
Worse: You're in it!

•••••

Bad: You find your children are sexually active.
Worse: With each other!

•••••

Bad: You come home and find your wife in bed with the mailman.
Worse: You're third in line!

•••••

Bad: You're caught having sex in a public place.
Worse: By your wife!

•••••

Bad: The dog licks your butt while you're having sex.
Worse: You like it!

Acknowledgments

Mike Oxbent and Harry P. Ness would like to thank the following people....

Nell Soars

Abe Iggcock

Alf Hucker

Anna Linjection

Avya Kutchukokoff (Russian shot putter)

Asheet Midrawz

Barry McCockiner

Ben Wackenoff

Buster Hymen

Clint Toris

Connie Lingus

Craven Moorhead

Dan Gleebitz

Dick Aiken

Dick Getzhard

Dick Gozinia

Dick Hurtz

Dick Likkah

Dick N. Cider

Dick Wacker

Dick Zucker

Didi Reelydoit

Don Keedik

E. Jack Ulation

Ella Vanass

Eric Shun

F. L. Aysheeo

Gena Talia
Gloria Stits
Gorden Shauers
Harry Balzac
Harry Muff
Harry Paratestes
Harry R. Sole
Haywood Jablowme
Herb Eaverstinks
Holden McGroin
Hope Tabonia
Hugh G. Rection
Hugh Jass
Hugh Jorgan
Ima Hoar
Isaac Hunt
Ivan Aiken Dick
Ivan Itchinanus
Ivana B. Laid
Ivana C. Cox
Ivor Biggun
Izzy Cumming
Jack Kanoff
Juan Kerr (well known Mexican bachelor)
Juan King (another well known Mexican bachelor)
Juan Nightstand
Liz Bean
Lou Briccant (a slippery customer)
Lou Sass
Martha Fokker
Master Bates
Matt Sterbator

Max E. Padd
May I. Tutchem
Mike Hunt
Mike Ockhurts
Mike Ocksmall
Mike Rack
Mike Rotchburns
Mya P. Nizhurtz
Oliver Cloesoff
Ophelia Balz
Pat McCrotch
Payne N. Diaz
Peter Gozenya
Phil Laysheo
Phil McCavity
Phil McCock
Phuck Yu (renowned Chinese diplomat)
Phyllis Schlong
R. Slicker
Ruben Mycock
Seaman Sample
Seymore Butts
Stacey Rhect
Stella Virgin
Tess Tickle
Titus Balsac
Torah Hyman
Uri Nate
Wilma Fingerdo
Yorik Hunt
Yousuckmynuts N. Scratchm
Yuban Wackinoff

Other Books from Ulysses Press

Atheist Universe: The Thinking Person's Answer to Christian Fundamentalism

David Mills, $14.95

Foreword by Dorion Sagan

Clear, concise, and persuasive, *Atheist Universe* details exactly why God is unnecessary to explain the universe and life's diversity, organization, and beauty.

Dirty Japanese: Everyday Slang from "What's Up?" to "F*ck Off!"

Seigo Nakao & Matt Fargo, $7.95

Even in traditionally minded Japan, slang from its edgy pop culture constantly enter into common usage. This book fills in the gap between how people really talk in Japan and what Japanese language students are taught.

The Happy Introvert: A Wild and Crazy Guide to Celebrating Your True Self

Elizabeth Wagele, $14.95

This fun, wacky handbook explores the richness introverts experience in their inner worlds and offers tips for enjoying life in an extroverted society.

In Your Jeans: A Pocket Guide to Your Changing Body

Wendy Darvill & Kelsey Powell, $9.95

Offers a safe, nonembarrassing way for preteens and teens to find answers on their own—without a lot of drama or preaching.

Mapping the Memory: Understanding Your Brain to Improve Your Memory

Rita Carter, $14.95

Helps readers reach a higher level of understanding about memory and how they can improve the working of their own brain function in this area.

MuggleNet.com's What Will Happen in Harry Potter 7: Who Lives, Who Dies, Who Falls in Love and How Will the Adventure Finally End?

Ben Schoen, Emerson Spartz, Andy Gordon, et al, $14.95

The experts at MuggleNet.com present a wide range of hard facts and bold predictions about the most popular storylines, favorite characters, and final outcome of the Harry Potter saga.

Serial Killers and Mass Murderers: Profiles of the World's Most Barbaric Criminals

Nigel Cawthorne, $12.95

Serial Killers and Mass Murderers present a fascinating investigation of the dark side.

Skater Girl: A Girl's Guide to Skateboarding

Patty Segovia & Rebecca Heller, $14.95

Reveals the ins and outs of skateboarding to young women who know that sporting some road rash is one off-the-hook lifestyle statement.

To order these books call 800-377-2542 or 510-601-8301, fax 510-601-8307, e-mail ulysses@ulyssespress.com, or write to Ulysses Press, P.O. Box 3440, Berkeley, CA 94703. All retail orders are shipped free of charge. California residents must include sales tax. Allow two to three weeks for delivery.